Teaching Is a Privilege

Twelve Essential Understandings for Beginning Teachers

Elizabeth Cervini Manvell

ROWMAN & LITTLEFIELD EDUCATION
A division of
ROWMAN & LITTLEFIELD PUBLISHERS, INC.
Lanham • New York • Toronto • Plymouth, UK

Published by Rowman & Littlefield Education
A division of Rowman & Littlefield Publishers, Inc.
A wholly owned subsidary of The Rowman & Littlefield Publishing Group, Inc.
4501 Forbes Boulevard, Suite 200, Lanham, Maryland 20706
http://www.rowmaneducation.com

Estover Road, Plymouth PL6 7PY, United Kingdom

British Library Cataloguing in Publication Information Available

Library of Congress Cataloging-in-Publication Data

Manvell, Elizabeth C., 1951-
  Teaching is a privilege : twelve essential understandings for beginning teachers / Elizabeth C.
Manvell.
     p. cm.
  Includes bibliographical references.
  ISBN 978-1-60709-109-7 (cloth : alk. paper) — ISBN 978-1-60709-110-3 (pbk. : alk. paper)
  — ISBN 978-1-60709-111-0 (electronic)
  1. Student teachers. 2. First year teachers. 3. Teachers—Professional relationships. 4. Teaching—
Philosophy. I. Title.
  LB2157.A3M34 2009
  370.71'1—dc22   2009021175

Printed in the United States of America

To Jason Hruscik, 1982–2008,
who had everything necessary
to become a memorable teacher.
His wise reflections grace the pages of this book.

Contents

Foreword

Elizabeth Manvell rightly brings the heart into the classroom. Effective leadership begins with respect and deep empathy for those who are led. If children are to love learning and love themselves, they must have a mirror that reflects that esteem and encourages their small steps toward self-efficacy and respectful treatment of others. Few beginning teachers want anything less for children, but teaching is difficult and intimidating to the neophyte, and classroom management too easily loses sight of the loftiest goals. Manvell sets out to replace fear and doubt with confidence and compassion; the effects reach far beyond the walls of the classroom. As teachers develop the self-knowledge and caring that nurtures academic learning in children, they also develop the integrity and humanity to educate children as persons and citizens.

Empathy and faith in children's abilities provides a sturdy foundation for a healthy classroom. Manvell knows, however, that it is not enough to merely teach compliance and self-control. An orderly environment for learning is necessary, but not sufficient to develop the skills citizens need in the twenty-first century. Every interaction in the classroom teaches a lesson: the social curriculum of the classroom shapes the life of the society, small and great.

To grow to adults able to fulfill their own dreams and be equally mindful of the needs and dreams of others, children must have opportunities to practice social skills. The richness of their experiences as they encounter different perspectives and cultures, share resources, and resolve conflicts develops them as citizens. Teachers literally are constructing the society as they go about managing purposeful social interaction in the classroom.

Manvell's perspective on beginning teachers is realistic. Her faith and compassion for their doubts and mistakes models the faith and compassion that good teachers extend to children. Elizabeth Manvell creates a better future for children and the society through her wise and loving guidance.

Dr. Joy Mosher, Ed.D.
Interim Director of Graduate Studies
SUNY Cortland

Preface

I have had this book in my head for a long time. Certain ideas continually rose to the forefront and nagged at me. They all revolved around how teachers view and relate to parents and students. I wanted to write a book so I could share my ideas about school climate and relationships with more people than the thirty student teachers I worked with each semester.

I thoroughly enjoyed working with my first-year teachers and my student teachers in their classrooms and at our seminars. They ranged from young college age to older second-career undergraduate and graduate students, and I was able to share in the excitement of their first opportunity to have their own class.

But amidst all their creativity and enthusiasm, sharp teaching skills, and dedication, I observed a subtle pattern of attitudes that intrigued me. My beginning teachers were often at a loss as to how to set a professional, yet reasonable and welcoming balance in their attitudes toward their students. No doubt they were full of good intentions, yet I knew their attitudes were blocking them from connecting on a sincere, caring, comfortable level with their students and their families. Unknowingly they put up artificial barriers between themselves and their students. Their attitudes surfaced at a range of intensities and revealed whether the new teachers saw themselves in a partnership with their students and families, or in a "them versus us" power struggle. It depended on how comfortable they were with their role as teacher.

A lack of confidence and self-reflection, and their resulting attitudes, manifested themselves in a variety of similar ways. Sometimes they surfaced as a negative view of parents, where the teachers would pass judgment on their parenting skills and blame them for the problems their children were having in the classroom. They also surfaced as frustration with those students who had behavior or learning problems, who after all the teachers' hard efforts still didn't "get it." From the teachers' perspective, they were sure their students would get it if they only paid attention and tried harder.

I came to understand that this attitude grew primarily from fear that their students would fail to learn and would misbehave. This perspective stemmed from a lack of understanding of individual differences and of the motivation behind behavior choices. They were also unaware of how what they did as teachers—what they said, their body language, and their choices in how to discipline—was a direct result of their own experiences, attitudes, and beliefs about society, parents, and accountability. These personal attitudes, in turn, had a direct influence on how they treated their students, and subsequently on how their students learned and behaved. Their lack of empathy and their tendency to see the child or parent as at fault concerned me. I firmly believed it didn't have to be this way—and shouldn't be. We needed to replace fear and doubt with confidence and compassion.

If we did not succeed in doing this, they were going to have a difficult time with classroom discipline, student motivation, and enlisting the help of parents. It would waste their teaching time and deplete their emotional and physical energy. It might even make them quit teaching. I believed this could be changed. I believed that I could help them take a step back and see things through a broader, more compassionate lens. And I believed that they were capable of changing their attitudes, beliefs, and teaching approaches to have more success with their students.

This book is my attempt to use what I learned from those beginning teachers to guide you to develop the self-knowledge and caring perspectives that will serve your students well, and to free you to have a rewarding and lengthy teaching career. I want you to always remember why you chose teaching.

Acknowledgments

This book is a culmination of my many years in the field of education. I thank all those I have worked with and learned from during my career, in particular the teachers I served as principal at Maine Memorial ES in upstate New York; my student teachers from the State University of New York at Cortland who shared a momentous time in their lives with me; the cooperating teachers who welcomed us into their classrooms and shared their expertise with patience and dedication; all the children who helped me and their beginning teachers understand what students need to be motivated, willing learners; and the parents who let me into their lives so we could help their children together. I also thank the Search Institute, who gave me their vote of confidence by allowing me to include a copy of their list "40 Developmental Assets for Middle Childhood" in this book. Their work has long been an inspiration to me and I wanted to share it with others.

Thank you to my colleagues and friends, Dr. Joy Mosher and Dr. Joan Koster, for reading the manuscript and giving it a thumb's up. I have great respect for their opinions.

Without an editor who thought others could benefit from my message there would be no book at all. I am forever indebted to Tom Koerner at Rowman & Littlefield Education for believing in me, and to Maera Stratton and Melissa McNitt for their upbeat guidance throughout this process.

There is a special place in my heart for the two dozen of my student teachers who graciously gave me permission to use their reflections. At a point in time we shared the privilege to teach, and their insights and moments of puzzlement and clarity continue to root my understandings in the real world.

I offer a heartfelt thank-you to my husband, Arthur Elfenbein, who supports me in my many educational endeavors and cheers me on through them all, including the writing of this book.

Introduction:
A Is for [a Positive] Attitude

WHAT AN OPPORTUNITY!

Have you thought about what motivated you to become a teacher? It might
have been the opportunity to do something personally satisfying and a desire
to be happy in your life's work. It could have been a love of children and a
belief that you could connect with them and make a difference in how their
lives turned out. It might have been the conviction that schools exert a powerful influence on the kind of people we send out into the world. Or maybe
you enjoyed school as a child and felt comfortable in that setting. All of these
likely had some influence on your decision.

We become teachers because, at our core, we believe all people are en-
titled to a productive, fulfilling life. Teaching is a chance to do something
professionally meaningful and personally rewarding to make this a reality. I
was blessed with an early passion for teaching and a thirst for understanding
human motivation and how people learn. Drawn to the challenging child and
driven by a strong sense of social justice, I believed in a teacher's circle of
influence and potential to have an impact on individuals and the educational
system. I wanted to be part of it.

The classroom was a place where I felt alive and inspired, and blessed to be
able to work with children. Along the way in my eclectic career in education,
I had opportunities to teach pre-kindergarten and elementary-age children,
college students, and older adults; serve as a school principal; work closely
with and train parents; and create syllabi for college teacher education classes
on student discipline, character education, and gender issues. The ultimate
prize of my career was the opportunity I ultimately had to supervise student
teachers in their field placements. This was where I could put everything I

1

had learned and believed into practice. As it turned out, student teaching was a life-changing field placement for me as well.

Working with pre-service teachers was a culmination of my journey, where it all came together for me. By this point, I knew a good teacher when I saw one, and I could identify the specific personal and professional qualities—*the dispositions*—critical for this success. When I read the National Council for Accreditation of Teacher Education (NCATE) definition of dispositions I knew I was on the right track.

> Professional dispositions [are] professional attitudes, values, and beliefs demonstrated through both verbal and non-verbal behaviors as educators interact with students, families, colleagues, and communities. These positive behaviors support student learning and development.
>
> —National Council for Accreditation of Teacher Education

TRANSLATING GOOD INTENTIONS TO GOOD OUTCOMES

Beginning teachers have enthusiasm and the best of intentions. Yet how do these intentions translate into the attitudes and behaviors that have the best outcomes for students? In many regards it happens when we put ourselves in our students' place and consider individual circumstances and needs.

> Good intentions . . .
>   A desire to do what is best
>   An open mind that considers the uniqueness of the situation
>   An empathetic view of the perspectives of the people involved
>   Wise choices based on the specifics . . .
>   Good outcomes

Implicit in this and all the essential understandings is a foundation of caring. In order to do this good work, teachers must care enough to try and to stick with it. It takes commitment and tenacity.

MENTORING BEGINNING TEACHERS

Teaching is about helping others grow and is dependent on trusting relationships. Everything we choose to do must be the right thing for students. Successful teachers:

- Help students evolve emotionally and socially
- Motivate each student to a high level of academic success
- Enlist the cooperation of families to help students achieve

- Are lifelong, reflective learners
- Are helpful, knowledgeable colleagues who advance the field of education
- Serve as positive role models for the school community
- Love their work and maintain an optimistic attitude

We can see how along with the instructional skills and knowledge of content, high on this list of dispositions is the kind of person you are and your attitudes toward your job, and the children and adults you work with.

This view that teaching is a product of attitude was always foremost in my mind as I mentored my student teachers. Before each semester began, we college supervisors would meet with our new students for an orientation session. As I spoke with my understandably anxious students for the first time, I would tell them that this was an auspicious and momentous occasion, that student teaching was the official beginning of their professional life. From this moment on, through what they said and did, they were establishing their reputation and professional work habits, and I wanted to help them get off to a good start. I could see a physical change in them immediately—they listened intently to what I was saying, and excitement and pride joined their nervousness. They realized they had made the transition from *student* to *teacher* and recognized the significance of that shift.

Now I wish to welcome *you* to the world of teaching and help you get off to a good start as well.

REFLECTION: FIFTH GRADE

Yesterday it struck me how comfortable I am in the front of the class. Last night when I was reflecting on my progress as a teacher, I realized just how far I have come. In the beginning I was very tense and nervous. I worried a great deal about how well I was going to be able to convey my knowledge of subjects to the students. Now, I am much more relaxed and I have a lot more fun teaching. I was very nervous in the beginning of this placement that I would not be any good at teaching and that my four years of college would have been a waste, but now I am able to see that they are paying off.

Today was the third day of my solo week without my cooperating teacher being in the classroom and it went extremely well. I am covering the content in the proper amount of time, and I am able to leave myself with a couple of minutes at the end of each lesson for students' questions. I am planning well in advance so that I am not being hammered with a massive amount of work each night. I am able to keep a positive atmosphere in the classroom at all times. Also, I am letting the students have fun, but pulling them back before things get out of control. Everything that we have talked about since the very first week I am noticing myself implementing into my teaching, and I could not imagine being anything else but a teacher.

TWO ROLES AT ONCE

Student teaching. What an interesting pairing of words. As a teacher you are a professional, looked up to by your students, expected to show confidence, and to be proficient in your instructional skills. At the same time you are a student facing a steep learning curve, who needs to work untiringly, and seek and try suggestions from your college supervisors, cooperating teachers, and school principal. The same is true of first-year teachers. If you do not take your role as a student thoughtfully and seriously, you will not succeed in your professional teaching capacity. If you do not keep an open mind and reflect on your practice, you will not succeed in your role as a learner. The two aspects nurture each other: The *teacher you* practices teaching and making decisions, and the *student you* evaluates, learns, and applies—all in a real-life situation, with real children.

This book can serve as an effective supplement to the training you received in your years of teaching preparation and to the guidance you receive from your supervisors and mentors. Under the best-case scenario, you read and discuss the essential understandings with others as you prepare to begin this life-changing personal and professional adventure. You might also read it on your own, consider it with an open mind, and ponder what you truly believe makes a successful teacher. In either case, the book will hopefully be a source of inspiration as you start your career, and something you refer to and reread throughout your life as a teacher.

WE NEED YOU!

We want you to have a long and satisfying career, but we are faced with the reality that beginning teachers have an alarming dropout rate. Some call it *exit attrition*, and it refers to those who leave teaching not because of a move or child rearing, and not to transfer to another school. It refers to those permanently leaving the profession for which they have trained hard and long, within their first few years. It is akin to dropping out of school.

This trend is costly in terms of dollars and wasted talent, and it is sad for the individuals involved. And as reported by the August 2005 Alliance for Excellent Education report on teacher attrition rates and causes, "Teacher Attrition: A Costly Loss to the Nation and to the States," it hits the poorer, lower-achieving schools the hardest. Here the impact is devastating, as students and their schools experience a revolving door of inexperienced teachers, never getting to enjoy the expertise and stability of a seasoned, confident, cohesive faculty.

It might sound simplistic to say that the key to your professional success as a teacher and to your personal contentment lies in the perspectives and attitudes you bring to your work. Yet, these personal dispositions are major influences on what keeps you in the classroom year after year, fresh and enthusiastic. They make your class the one that students hope for and the one that parents want their children to experience. With a positive attitude and empathetic perspective, you have a better chance of avoiding teacher burnout and having a long, satisfying career in education. You might even decide to move on to a position in school administration, where we need talented, optimistic leaders. The beauty is that in the process, you bless hundreds of students with an uplifting school experience.

Thinking Activity: What's Next?

Try this power writing activity. Make a T-chart with the word *Joys* on one side and *Challenges* on the other. Set a timer for one minute and write as many teaching joys as you can think of before the timer goes off. Set the timer again and repeat with teaching challenges. The object is to write down your ideas as fast as they pop into your head. It is similar to a game of Boggle, where you have to make as many words as you can from the letters that are showing before time is up. Keep these joys and challenges in mind as you process the twelve Essential Understandings.

REFLECTION: THIRD GRADE

Today for math instead of practice sheets, I put them into small groups of two or three and gave each group multiplication flash cards. Each group had three minutes with each set of flash cards, and then they switched to the next group. The key was to help them memorize. Then later we played conductor with the cards. The kids loved it! I noticed a huge improvement in memorization. We played it three times throughout the day. Also, I had my fair share of injuries and tears today. In the morning A.'s loose tooth started to bleed, K. started crying on the way to art over something she wouldn't tell me, P. started crying because she didn't want anyone to know her middle name, R. got a bloody nose during science, and D. started crying because he thought he was having an asthma attack. So, it was a very interesting day!

A JOY AND A CHALLENGE

The reality is that teaching is both a joy and a challenge. It is exhilarating and heartbreaking, inspirational and exhausting. There is no other job quite like it. It is all these disparate things because you are working with children and are expected to be a people mover and a miracle worker, and you do not get to choose which children you teach. It is one of the toughest jobs you could have because human nature tells us it isn't easy to get people to change. Your job is to take children from one point in their development and guide them to continually higher levels. Actually, a teacher's job is not just to get students to change; it is to get them to *want* to change!

This is amazingly hard work and also a source of tremendous satisfaction. Those who thrive in the classroom can handle the challenges and find the joy, day after day, year after year. They have a positive, can-do attitude that is noticeable in whatever they do.

Such positive personal qualities are a major factor in the hiring process. School administrators and hiring teams look for the candidate who is strong in child development and in curriculum, instruction, assessment, and state and national standards, and they also look for a person who has an upbeat nature and shows a special spark. They want you to be intelligent and articulate *and* have a positive attitude and warm personality. They want you to convey a genuine passion for the content you teach *and* a firm commitment to meeting the emotional, social, and academic needs of all children. They want you to have a pragmatic approach to classroom management *and* still be able to create a welcoming classroom climate.

The bottom line is they are hoping to see an aspiring teacher who has it all—a positive outlook and palpable enthusiasm to go along with that strong set of instructional and management skills. In my experience interviewing prospective teachers, if we found a person with these special qualities, we had something to be excited about because we knew this array of dispositions makes for a memorable, effective teacher—one with longevity. We could teach a new teacher the school curriculum and how to enter the attendance into the computer each morning, but we were well aware that it wasn't as easy to teach new teachers to be spirited, kind teachers and school leaders. For this they needed to have taken an honest look at themselves to discover who they really were and what they truly stood for, and then be willing and eager to build from that point. This is my hope for you as you start your career, for you to be that kind of professional.

REFLECTION: FIRST GRADE

I love the fact that the saying "Time flies when you're having fun" really rings true for me at this placement and with teaching in general. I have worked other jobs that have not been fulfilling and have made the days drag on forever and ever. Now that I am in the classroom and teaching, the days just fly by. Also I feel so comfortable and content. I do not come home and stress about what I will have to do tomorrow. I am finally confident and comfortable with what I am doing and why I am doing it.

My lesson went well today. I was very nervous today before I started. I am not sure exactly why but I think it has to do with starting at a new placement and teaching new students for the first time. I want to succeed and ensure that they are having fun and learning and the first time is difficult. I think as time goes on it gets easier. I am excited to look at their work and see the results of my lesson.

WHY DO YOU LEAVE?

We have mentioned some of the reasons why you might have chosen teaching as your profession. This reflection captures some of that magic. But how do so many beginning teachers go from such a hopeful view to leaving teaching for good? How does this disappointing shift happen?

Among other factors, I have identified two common issues that contribute to the high attrition rate of beginning teachers—classroom discipline and dealing with parents, coupled with content to master and time pressures. I observed this myself, and my heart goes out to student and first-year teachers as they juggle the cognitive (hard) and affective (soft) realms of teaching and squeeze it all into a too-jam-packed teaching day.

It is not surprising that new teachers get discouraged. We do them a grave disservice when we put them in a classroom situation without preparing them for both challenges. Students in my college's elementary education program were lucky to have an entire course dedicated to classroom discipline and social responsibility, and I was lucky to be able to teach it at the undergraduate and graduate levels. It was an essential component of teacher preparation and deserved its own course. Designing and teaching the course caused me to process and solidify my own beliefs about discipline so I could guide others to that same level of self-understanding and confidence that what they were doing was right.

As part of teacher preparation, we need courses that require prospective teachers to think critically about core personal issues and understand how these relate to their attitudes. Relationships are the foundation of the teacher-student, teacher-family dynamic and in my opinion trump many cognitive teaching skills in payoff. If you haven't processed this internally and then honed these realizations into a belief system and set of behaviors you can put into action in the classroom, you are at a distinct disadvantage coming out of the starting block. You are also at higher risk of job stress and teacher burnout.

GETTING THE MOST FROM THIS BOOK

Over time, it became apparent to me that these twelve Essential Understandings were the foundation of teacher success and satisfaction. The Essential Understandings are what I think of as the softer side of teaching, the personal qualities and relationships you build that allow you to use your instructional teaching skills to their maximum — and to be happy in your work. This book focuses on these softer dispositions because I have seen how they can make or break you as a new teacher, how critical they are if we are to teach the diverse students in our schools, if we are to model tolerance and respect, and if we are to foster a commitment to social justice, all in a climate of interconnectedness and shared responsibility.

I fear this critical softer side of teaching is not stressed sufficiently in many pre-service teacher education programs and schools, especially with the emphasis on academic testing, performance standards, assessment strategies, and accountability. With this narrow focus comes the proliferation of pre-packaged, lock-step instructional programs that take the "teacher" out of the "teaching." They are designed to be foolproof (teacher-proof), delivered in the same manner, with the same narrative, using the same materials, and at the same pace regardless of the student audience, the talents of the teacher, and the essential understandings highlighted in this book.

Contrary to this narrow definition of teaching, attitudes and relationships serve as the underlying themes of *Teaching Is a Privilege*. This book leads you through a set of Essential Understandings that nurture a positive, accepting, realistic attitude toward students and families, and an acceptance of responsibility for what happens in your classroom. Once internalized, these understandings give you the tools to create a classroom climate conducive to learning.

When you look for a teaching position, they also make you shine in an interview, help you land a teaching job, and equip you with the vision and skills to make you a memorable, inspirational teacher who stays in the profession. When you are done reading this book, you will have the self-assurance that comes from self-knowledge and a deeply rooted belief system that drives your thinking. And you will also have practical manifestations of your beliefs to apply right away to your classroom.

As you explore these understandings, notice that they overlap in concepts and principles. This is to be expected and is, in fact, reassuring. The redundancy reinforces the position that teaching is not merely a set of discrete skills to memorize; it is an individual's holistic view of children and adults, an array of intertwined beliefs, knowledge, and behaviors. My goal is for you to go beyond a philosophy of teaching that is often little more than a generic statement lacking much substance, to a well-thought-out belief system supported by specific ways to incorporate it into your professional life . . . every day, all the time, with everyone.

The charm is that belief systems stay with you over time. They are core to who you are and what you stand for, a compass to guide your decision making. You may need to learn how to teach multiplication with decimals or what constitutes a primary resource, but you never forget what you believe in. It would be like forgetting your name. Beliefs help you navigate this complicated world and its challenges, giving you the direction and confidence to take a stand and try. They become second nature.

To enrich the discussions about the twelve Essential Understandings, I have received permission from a dozen of my former student teachers to use actual journal entries they wrote during their classroom field placements. These real-life reflections from the heart reveal the thinking process they went through as they worked with students and their families as professionals for the first time. They show the joys and challenges, the exhilaration and heartbreak, the exhaustion and inspiration of what feels like a daunting task. They provide a window into what these beginning teachers wrestled with as they developed into true professionals.

TAKE YOUR TIME

As you read through the twelve Essential Understandings, take time to think about the concepts, answer the questions posed, and complete the thinking activities provided. Personal interaction with the concepts is the way you effect true change in your heart and mind, and come out a more compassionate and prepared teacher. This allows you to internalize the Essential Understandings in a way that makes sense to you.

You will be asked to think seriously and honestly about what you believe about children, schools, families, discipline, and responsibility. You might be asked to reconsider some long-held assumptions and unchallenged habits with the intent to develop a working set of conscious beliefs and principles. These understandings give you a clearer lens through which to view all your interactions and help guide your choices. Then you are ready to apply them in an intentional, consistent way.

Invest the time and effort to do the thinking exercises included. They are instrumental if you are to develop an intrinsic level of personal understanding. As with the children you will soon teach, we learn best that which is relevant to us personally and that which we can experience firsthand. This is true regardless of the grade level or academic discipline you teach, and it is true when you read this book and when you have your own students to teach. It is the rationale behind getting education students out of the college classroom into the real world where they can take what they know and believe and try it with real children. It is also the motivation behind mentoring programs for first-year teachers and continuing professional development for all teachers.

—∞∞∞—

Thinking Activity: Your Quality Teaching Experience

Before you go any further, take a few minutes to write down a description of what you want your first classroom teaching experience to be like. List the things you want to happen there. Now take these hopes and tuck them away in the back of this book. As you read the book and do the thinking activities, you will begin to realize how much power you truly have to establish the kind of teaching experience and teaching career you dream of having.

—∞∞∞—

Now let's begin this transformational journey through the twelve Essential Understandings. I am privileged to be your guide.

Essential Understanding 1

Teaching Is a Privilege: Show You Are Worthy of the Responsibility

---

REFLECTION: FIFTH GRADE

Today was very strange because I was out of the classroom a lot. I missed it. I spent the morning doing one lesson plan and visiting classrooms in the intermediate building. I think the best part of the day was returning to my classroom and having all my kids cheer because I had returned. It made me feel like I have really done a good job connecting with them so that they are happy to see me. I remember having teachers I was not happy to see and I am glad I am not one of them.

THE LEAP OF FAITH

Parents, may I borrow your children, just for a while—say, five days a week, six hours a day? May I have them for thirteen years? You can have them back each night and in the summer . . . unless, that is, they need to go to summer school.

That's right. Teachers are in the business of borrowing other people's children! The children are on loan to the school system and put in your care. Parents are expected to give their children to us in good faith. They do not have a choice unless they opt to homeschool them. How will you prove you are worthy of their trust? One way is to ask yourself how you wanted to be treated when you were a child in school and, if you are also a parent, how you want your own child to be treated by a teacher.

One of the first things I told my student teachers as they headed out to practice-teach was that, contrary to what it might seem at times, students are not there to make their life as a teacher easy *or* difficult. They are just there, in all their various forms, and with all their various talents and frailties. Children are who they are, and by becoming teachers we tacitly agree to accept and embrace this diversity along with the responsibility to better their lives. I told my students this because they were trained, soon-to-be-licensed teaching professionals, and I believe teaching other people's children is a privilege we all should take seriously. It isn't even a choice. It is what our profession and society rightfully expect of us.

REFLECTION: SIXTH GRADE

Today was a very emotional day for me. Throughout this placement I have been lucky enough to be surrounded by amazing people. All of the teachers were very personable and easy to get along with. I feel like I have grown to form bonds with many members of the faculty, which has made my time there more enjoyable. I have also formed a strong bond with the students. It was very difficult to leave them today for the last time. The difficulty level can be compared to saying goodbye to friends at the end of the summer when everyone is going back to college. I could tell that it was tough for the students to say goodbye because many of them looked upset as they were thanking me for teaching them and making learning a fun experience.

At the end of the day I thanked the students for allowing me to come into their classroom and teach them. I told them how much I valued each and every one of them and will miss coming in each day and seeing them.

This morning, I received what I consider to be the best compliment that I have ever received. A mother dropped off her daughter at school and walked her to the classroom. Immediately, the mother thanked me for the excellent job that I did teaching her daughter. She told me that each day her daughter would go home and tell her how I made each day fun, and the way I taught made her daughter enjoy school and more eager to learn. That compliment alone showed me that no matter what faults I may have had throughout my time in this school, I still accomplished a goal of any teacher. That goal is to be able to reach students in a way that makes them look forward to coming to school and makes students want to learn. This mother made me feel like I am in the right professional field and am on the right track to becoming an effective teacher. This mother's comments are something that I will never forget for the rest of my teaching career.

IN LOCO PARENTIS

It is safe to say there is nothing parents hold more precious than their children, and they must, by law, entrust them physically and emotionally to virtual strangers (also known as "schoolteachers") for most of their waking hours, for a sequence of months and years. Throughout this book, the term *parents* refers to the array of family situations where children are raised by one or two biological parents, guardians, grandparents, adoptive parents, same-sex partners, foster care providers, stepparents, and primary caregivers. This array should be acknowledged and accommodated. To this list of society's caregivers we can add teachers, who, it is interesting to note, by law are said to serve in "in loco parentis"—in the position or place of a parent—and are expected to do what a reasonable parent would do in any given situation.

This is the leap of faith that mothers and fathers, guardians, and grandparents must make. They must believe that teachers have their children's best interests at heart, and at the same time realize that teachers are also obligated to follow their professional judgment and adhere to the policies and practices, mandates and regulations of the federal government, their state education department and school district, and their particular school and grade level. What a moral and intellectual responsibility this places on teachers. A good teacher not only covers skills and content, a good teacher also worries about what parents worry about: the children's social and emotional adjustment, their ability to make good decisions, their mental and physical well-being, and their future as self-sufficient, contributing adults. This is an enormous responsibility *and* a privilege.

I know how personal and deeply rooted is this desire to protect our children. As my own children went through the public school system I wanted teachers to see them as unique people, and to pay attention to each one's welfare as a whole child. I had an advantage. I was a teacher, armed with the perspectives of both sides of the parent-teacher relationship, and I knew how to navigate the world of schools. Most parents do not have this luxury. This is why I came to believe that teaching is a special privilege and that good teachers should make sure parents understand that they take their teaching responsibilities seriously.

As a teacher and principal, my goal was for parents to know I personally valued them and their children, and respected their dreams for their children. When they didn't have dreams, I showed them what was possible. I recognized their struggles and fears and wanted them to know I felt privileged to help them raise their children. And I knew I had to earn, not merely expect, their trust. This approach to parents rarely, if ever, failed me. That is not to say there weren't trying situations that tested my resolve, especially when I was a principal, yet it surely made those situations less antagonistic and more optimistic. How could parents be antagonistic toward a confident, approachable teacher or administrator who *shows she truly cares about their child*? In like kind, it is difficult to be antagonistic toward struggling parents once you have put yourself in their place and understand their personal motivations and perspectives.

REFLECTION: PRE-K

Today was a fairly easy day because it was the last day before winter break. My first winter break in a high-needs school, however, brought up many questions for me. I wondered how many of our students would spend most of the break hungry without being fed breakfast and lunch at the school. I wondered if there would be proper supervision throughout the week or if many of the young children would be left with older brothers and sisters while moms and dads headed off to work.

I also wondered how many of the parents viewed this extra break as a burden instead of the welcomed vacation many of the teachers raved about. The thing I worried about the most, though, was that many of these students might not hear how wonderful, smart, or valuable they are until they return to school next Monday. Perhaps, more than at any other school, a high-needs school must work diligently to build a strong school-family relationship so that the needs of the students and families can be met.

This brought me to another message I wanted to convey to teachers—that the vast majority of parents love and are concerned about their children even if it doesn't always look that way, even when they disagree with us, and even when they seem not to care. We need teachers who live by this belief, who respect parents and welcome them and their children with empathy and compassion, regardless of their situation in life, their dress, their speech, or their attitude toward school and us. Together, parents and teachers get to prepare our country's future citizens, influence our communities, and steer the direction the world takes. What other profession can say that? This is the profound privilege parents and teachers share.

DO NO HARM

This is a true story. When my daughter was in kindergarten she drew an elaborate, colorful picture for her teacher. She carefully wrote her name on it and brought it to school. That afternoon, when she returned home, she stomped in, obviously upset. "I'm never going to do that again," she told me.

"Do what?" I asked her.

"Give her anything again. She took my picture and then she put it in the garbage."

My jaw dropped. She threw it in the garbage? I knew she was a stern teacher but I could not believe she was so lacking in empathy. This was the antithesis of my concept of what a teacher should be. With this one act she had broken most of the basic principles of human relationships, and she had deeply hurt my child's feelings in the process. Here it was only kindergarten and my daughter now had a negative feeling toward teachers. And, unfortunately, I was now uncomfortable leaving my child in her care.

I decided to send the teacher a brief note explaining the ramifications of what she had done by this one thoughtless act. I worked hard to keep the tone of the letter respectful and hopeful. In my heart and mind I was upset to know that the person I must trust with my most precious possession had mistreated my child. I wondered about the hurtful things she did to the other children, things their parents would never find out about.

And then, many years later, I read the following reflection from one of my student teachers that reminded me of this incident, and I was reassured that for the most part, our children are in good hands.

REFLECTION: SECOND GRADE

One thing that I am really starting to notice about students in the younger grades is that they love drawing and coloring pictures for their teacher. I have a huge stack of pictures that students drew for me sitting at home on my desk. I value each one because seeing them drawing and coloring pictures for me shows me that they like me teaching them.

Thinking Activity: How Do I Reassure You?

Please stop reading for a minute. Imagine it is September and a new school year has just begun for you. Write a brief letter to the parents of your students reassuring them that you will take good care of their children while they are in your care.

What did you say to reassure them? What did you promise to do? I imagine it was not very difficult to express yourself so that parents would be comforted.

As this activity illustrates, the privileges of parenting and teaching come with a tremendous amount of responsibility that requires an investment of time and a sustained, thoughtful effort. The job of parents is to keep their children safe, show them love and caring concern, and teach them about life and what it means to be a responsible, capable person. A critical factor in their success is defining a comfort zone between permissiveness and rigid control. This comfort zone creates the healthy home environment that parents aim to set for their children.

Similarly, in your role as a teacher, you are expected to keep your students safe at all times, show them you care about them as individuals, and facilitate their personal and intellectual growth. A critical factor in your success is your ability to establish a professional balance between being the students' friend and being their warden. This comfort zone is the positive classroom climate and healthy adult-child relationship you strive for. People—parents and children, spouses and friends, colleagues and administrators, and teachers and students—can weather bad times and share good times if the relationship is in balance, with mutual respect, trust, and a healthy dose of honest, regular communication.

REFLECTION: FIFTH GRADE

What went well: Today there was a substitute teacher in the classroom. He had been a teacher here for 30+ years and was back for the day. He is a big guy with a booming voice and gentle manner and the students loved him. I learned a great deal about keeping the class moving forward in a gentle and firm way. I tried to help as much as I could and I noticed that at the end of the day he had left a note for the teacher saying that "the student teacher was a big help." I felt great about that.

SMILING IS A *GOOD* THING

"Don't smile until Halloween." I cringe whenever I hear this cynical and misleading piece of advice that is sometimes offered to nervous beginning teachers. They are cautioned to present themselves to their students in a stern, no-nonsense manner. Not only is this bad advice, unless you are humorless and always in total control, it isn't even possible.

In the same teacher-centered, adversarial frame of mind, beginning teachers are advised to decide on and make (and laminate, so they can use it year after year) a neatly printed chart of classroom rules and binding consequences to post and review with their students the first day. Again, this advice is not only *not* helpful, it is damaging—because it tells impressionable new teachers, anxious to keep order in the classroom (the thing they worry about most), to disregard the human side of classroom management and student achievement, the caring working relationship you wish to develop with your students. This relationship is an investment with no place for shortcuts.

When you ask about classroom management, more fitting advice would be that thriving in the classroom is predicated on the following: having high, realistic, articulated standards for behavior; coming to class every day prepared with well-thought-out lesson plans designed to engage your students; being able to put yourself in your students' places when you discipline, applying basic principles of accountability with respect and dignity; and letting your genuine enthusiasm and personality shine through. That is how you win over students and establish a productive learning community. Smiling is mandatory.

You will eventually learn the grade-level curriculum and how to plan thoroughly and develop a lesson to fit within a certain timeframe. You will learn how to organize your materials and the flow of the school day, and then with flexibility and good humor deal with interruptions to your teaching. You will learn to navigate a system where uninterrupted teaching time is precious and rare. Without a productive, mutually respectful relationship with your students, much of your time and energy goes toward managing them and merely getting through the day, with instruction and student learning a distant second and third.

When you first meet your students, immediately establish yourself as an adult who gives respect and expects respect. You can do this by the manner in which you speak to them, by the way you listen to them, and by being prepared and openly excited to teach. As we noted before, this is the same balance—the comfort zone—that successful parents strike as they raise their children.

Some teaching dispositions are akin to what any dedicated professional, in any field, who has a positive attitude and drive to be successful would do: being accountable and open to suggestions and new ideas; showing you are serious by dressing appropriately for your role; showing initiative by help-ing out; volunteering to take on additional responsibilities; and developing respectful relationships with coworkers. This is the concept of going beyond what is expected of you to the unexpected and the appreciated.

Teachers, by the delicate nature of our profession, are working with virtu-ally defenseless children, and therefore must live by an even higher moral and ethical standard. Children are placed in our hands and depend on us to take good care of them. We have the power to elevate or break their spirits, to believe in them or cast them off, to accept them as they are or reject them for what they are not, to never give up on them or to write them off. As teach-ers we have to move past our own insecurities and biases to a frame of mind where we always put children first as we faithfully demonstrate a commit-ment to preserving their dignity and meeting their needs.

Achieving this level of accountability and dedication, delivered with a positive, hopeful attitude, is how you show parents and the world you are worthy of the privilege to teach. These qualities manifest themselves in the way your classroom *feels*—the climate you create—which is the subject of Essential Understanding 2.

Essential Understanding 2

Your Attitude Sets the Tone for the Classroom: Create a Positive and Secure Learning Climate

REFLECTION: FIFTH GRADE

I found today's seminar especially rewarding because questions I did not realize I had were brought to the surface. It was also interesting to hear other student teachers' thoughts and concerns about similar topics with different outcomes. We are learning from each other. Thank you for creating a safe environment for us to share.

CAUSE AND EFFECT

This reflection meant a lot to me personally and professionally. It told me I was successfully setting the learning climate I intended to create. The impact of a safe environment is based on a simple concept: How students feel about you and your classroom affects how well they do in your classroom, and impacts your chances of being a successful teacher. It is all about establishing and maintaining healthy relationships through the heart and soul of a caring adult. So the first thing is to establish a respectful, secure learning climate.

School is a place you go when you need to learn something. By definition, learning requires taking risks because you are leaving the safe and familiar as you move from a state of unknowing to a state of knowing. This puts the learner in a vulnerable position. Taking a risk means having the courage to put yourself on the line, where you may be harmed or unsuccessful. We are best able to do this when we believe in ourselves and know others are supporting us as we try.

The concept that risk taking is at the core of learning applies to students in your classrooms as well as to you in your role as a new teacher. You are taking risks as you learn to teach and you, too, deserve a safe place to try. Consider how the attitudes and approaches your college supervisor, cooperating teachers, and the principal and staff of the schools where you work will affect your experience! Cardinal Newman, a British preacher who lived from 1801 to 1890, expressed it this way so long ago: "A man would do nothing, if he waited until he could do it so well that no one would find fault with what he has done." He had the soul of a teacher.

Take a look back to what you wrote for Essential Understanding 1. What did you say you wanted from your teaching experience? Likely one thing you wanted was a supportive environment in which to learn how to be a good teacher, with people who understood that you were *learning*. You deserve supervisors who approach their mentoring role believing in you and all the good that can happen—in other words, they model an optimistic, can-do attitude. Whatever the situation, people tend to see what they are looking for and they often wind up getting what they are expecting. The lens they look through determines how they experience life.

If you approach teaching with the attitude that students are a problem, that they don't listen, have no manners, don't want to learn, and that society and their parents have ruined them, you interpret all that happens in this light. If you believe that they are precious human beings, inherently good, impressionable and vulnerable, and that they are here to learn and you are here to meet them wherever they are, you see all the positives, the growth, the breakthroughs, and the sometimes-ever-so-slight, continuous progress. Nowhere is this optimistic attitude more important than in what goes on between a teacher and a student in a school classroom.

There are constructive and destructive ways to give feedback and make suggestions. You have probably experienced both in your life. Just think about the transformational power of a genuine smile and an unexpected kind word from a supervisor. My student teachers and non-tenured teachers amazed me with the learning activities they planned for my observations. It took confidence and trust on their part to lead an open-ended discussion or to let the students work in groups, or to use interesting and sometimes messy materials. The greatest compliment I received as a supervisor and principal was their willingness to take these risks and their excitement for me to observe and critique their lessons. The more welcoming and safe a climate I provided, the more they would take risks, experiment with new ideas, and grow from the experience. This sounds like the definition of a positive classroom climate, and it is.

A CAPTIVE AUDIENCE

We have established that, by law, every child in the United States must go to school. This is both a basic right and also a necessity if we are to educate people to be active participants in a well-functioning democracy. Consider this: The elementary and secondary school years are the one common, sustained cultural experience that all of our nation's children share. Compulsory education is a blessing because it provides teachers with the opportunity to impact every child individually and whole generations collectively. There is no question that we have a lot to accomplish in those thirteen years.

For some, school is the first and last time they are part of an organized social group. While we have the chance, public education has to avail itself of this remarkable opportunity and honor its moral imperative to teach our children to be smart *and* good people. How do we teach them to be both smart and good? We do this when we intentionally provide them with a learning environment free from harassment, ridicule, intolerance, and physical violence, where expectations are high and clear and support is plentiful, where their ideas and individuality are welcomed, and pro-social skills are nurtured. As we said before, schools, like families, have the power to create just such a secure environment for their children. It is quite an impressive opportunity and, because we also realize that children are a captive audience, we must treat them with loving concern and compassion as we do this.

THE POWER OF FEELING SAFE

Learning requires risk taking, and we cannot take risks if we do not feel safe and cared for. Embarrassment and fear are paralyzers. Trying the unknown (*learning*) can be intimidating for children. For adults, too! Simply put, no matter what our age, we work hard for people we care about and respect, and we care about and respect people who care about and respect us. In other words, you get what you give when you create a cycle of trust and good turns.

REFLECTION: THIRD GRADE

My beliefs have definitely been reinforced that behavioral issues take up a lot of time and consideration. If there were none, the day would be so much more productive. School is not only about learning the subjects but it is actually (at the early ages) learning how to act and what is acceptable behavior. This is especially true if the student does not get much support at home. The trick is to blend it into a lesson without it seeming like you are constantly "speaking to" certain students or complaining about their behavior. This is a huge challenge. I find myself wondering more often about how I can get certain students to pay attention or not disrupt everyone else than I do about what I am actually trying to teach. I think that balancing the two is the real challenge.

When our students step on the school bus or pass through the classroom door, they count on us to make sure they are valued and protected. They should expect to be treated well and should know that they are expected to treat others the same way. With this sense of belonging and security, and with clear parameters for behavior, grows the courage to take emotional, psychological, social, and intellectual risks and to rally from setbacks. In such a climate, children learn what they are capable of and gain confidence that they have something important to contribute. They develop the inner strength to make good choices and the motivation to treat each other better. This is the real foundation for learning and the basis of a good education. This safe and secure school climate helps us raise smart *and* good kids, and this is what we, and the rest of society, say we want.

School climate is how our school feels to us as it defines our place in the school subculture. School climate shows in the way we treat people and property. It is the product of the relationships among members and it affects the level of respect, achievement, and cooperation a school enjoys. It is also true that school climate is a factor in the amount of disrespect, apathy, and violence a school must deal with. Children behave and learn better, and teachers teach better, in schools where they feel safe, supported, and respected, and where a sense of humor can carry the day. It all comes down to this basic question: Is our school a place where it is safe and enjoyable for *all* students and staff to live and learn?

Every building, room, and natural space has an emotional climate that evokes a feeling in us. Your reaction to a place or situation is a product of your prior experiences or lack of exposure. Think about how you feel when you walk through the door of your favorite restaurant or through the door of your workplace. How do you feel when you visit a park or the town where you grew up? How about when you visit someone's home for the first time? Do these places feel safe and welcoming, or foreign and unfriendly to you? Do they feel the same to everyone who enters? Many factors might affect your view: the people you encounter; how much money you have; the language you speak; the clothes you wear; and most importantly, what your experience there, or in a similar place, was like.

Schools and classrooms have their own unique culture that sets the tone for everything that happens. As the teacher, you control the climate. You can provide a hesitant child or a disenfranchised parent with a new, positive view of school and teachers. How could we justify doing anything less? What a sad state of affairs it would be if schools were not committed to making sure they are hospitable places. We serve the public and society, so the least we can do is to embrace our students and their families.

REFLECTION: FOURTH GRADE

Today was not a day for dealing with academic issues but rather a day of discussing kindness and differences. In social studies I made a point to cover the differences among people and the uniqueness that each person brings to every situation. I feel this was the highlight of my lesson. However, there are greater issues that have surfaced beyond the knowledge of my cooperating teacher and me.

A parent phone call to our school made it apparent that two students in our class are forming some type of hate group. The target of their hate was not established but no matter what, this is a pressing issue for all children. The school psychologist made a stop at the classroom today to address the issue. I was aware that she was coming so I decided to work the same type of discussion into social studies. It makes me so sad to see children hurting one another. It is my goal to reinforce acceptance and tolerance each and every day. I want these children to enter adolescence and adulthood with kind hearts and open minds.

We have been talking about a school as a home, a close community where, under caring adult supervision, children practice making choices and learning skills to get along with others and to be independent. As I read this reflection I kept saying to myself, "Yes, yes, yes! This is our mission." School, like home, is a place where adult mentors help students learn about who they are, what they are capable of, and what society expects from them. Intentionally or not, this is what is happening in both the family and school arenas, so why not intentionally make your classroom climate welcoming and challenging?

Many factors contribute to the security of a school and the degree of connectedness students feel:

- The relationships members have with each other
- The level of trust and communication that exists among staff, parents, and students
- The clarity and fairness of policies
- The level of respect for differences
- The behaviors and attitudes that are encouraged, tolerated, forbidden, and ignored

Without that connectedness, members of the school community can be fragmented and feel insecure because they know that without a common vision to bind us together, anything can happen.

Climate building takes work if you want to do it with purpose and a clear vision. A positive learning climate isn't something that just happens, and school climate is not static. As is true with all relationships, the climate is subject to change and, therefore, demands that we tend to it regularly and constantly ask what messages our policies and behaviors send to the members of our school community. We need to assess what we are doing, consciously or unconsciously, to ensure that the dignity and safety of each child, parent, teacher, aide, bus driver, cafeteria worker, custodian, principal, and volunteer is protected.

Thinking Activity: How Does It Feel?

This can be done using an informal climate assessment. Make a list of the staff in your building and the students in your classroom. As you get to know a person, jot down what it must feel like being that person in your school. As you gather information, look for patterns and trends. Assess how appreciation and consideration are bestowed on that person. In doing this simple exercise you will discover that the experience is not the same for every member of the school community. Your job is to sort out how individual students are doing, what is going well, and what should be improved in your school and classroom.

YOU'VE ALREADY HAD GOOD TRAINING

You might not have realized that you already have a wealth of information about what *to do* and *not to do* stored in your memory. Unlike other professions, everyone who enters the teaching profession has had sixteen-plus years of firsthand experience in the system! Reach inside and put this valuable resource to good use.

Thinking Activity: When I Was a Kid . . .

Think back to your own childhood experiences as a student, preferably the age level you are preparing to teach. Think about what you liked and what really bothered you. Picture yourself as a child and think why you felt that way. Write your ideas on the following chart. For example, if I were doing this exercise I might think of my sixth-grade classroom, where I liked being

When I was a Kid in School. . .

What I liked	What I didn't like
Feelings these caused	Feelings these caused

allowed to work on projects with a small group out in the hall because it gave me freedom and a chance to talk and be creative. I also might recall how I did not like it when this same teacher punished the whole class with a surprise test when only a few kids were fooling around. Now it is your turn to recall what you did and did not like . . .

What kind of things did you recall? Did the associated feelings come back? Did certain teachers stand out as memorable, while you wish you had never had some of them? Take this insight and apply it to the way you interact with your students. *Rule of thumb*: "I didn't like it when I was in school so I won't do it to my students." Make it your motto, the foundation for creating a classroom climate that is purposefully inviting for students.

Now share these findings with others and listen to their perspectives. You likely discovered universal experiences most did like (free time, coloring, being read to) and most didn't like (copying notes from the board, yelling, teachers punishing the whole class). This is valuable information you can use as you make decisions about your own classroom. Yet there is a twist.

You probably also found differences in what your peers liked and didn't like. While you might have loved recess because you were a good athlete and popular, the teacher sitting next to you might have hated it because she was teased and excluded. Look at the implications of these differences. While you couldn't wait to get outside, she got a pit in her stomach every morning just thinking about it. The primitive fight-or-flight part of the brain was at work, and feelings like this likely interfered with her ability to participate fully and learn.

A limbic system on alert overrides the frontal lobe of the brain where reasoning and processing happen. If I am afraid of spiders and you are afraid of snakes, we each click into panic mode when confronted with the source of our fear. In the presence of something scary, that is all we can think of. Both fears should be acknowledged and each of us treated accordingly.

This illustrates the principle that since people do not all have the same history and share the same perceptions and feelings, we should, in kind, avoid assuming things about children. We have to observe and ask to truly know someone. *Second rule of thumb*: I need to get to know my students and what they are all about, and treat them accordingly.

Another practice has a profound effect on the classroom climate we create for our students. It relates to competition and being put on the spot. One child might love spelling bees (usually the best speller) while many find them just one more opportunity to fail—with an audience. Which were you? Would you like to participate in a spelling bee now in your college classroom or at a faculty meeting? How good are you at spelling out loud? What an eye-opener. Ask around and see what other people think. The diversity of responses might make you think differently about competitive games that pit one child or a group of students against one another.

People have different perspectives and feelings, likes and dislikes. Keeping these broad understandings of human nature and motivation in mind ensures you consider each child as an individual as you plan learning activities. It may even motivate you to eliminate spelling bees and the like from your instructional repertoire altogether. Unless, that is, it is an optional, fun activity for self-selected students who like that sort of thing. There surely is no justification to use a spelling bee for instructional purposes.

More effective and considerate ways exist to teach spelling, such as through the students' own writing. You will read more about this in Essential Understanding 10, where we discuss how important it is to have a valid reason for everything you do.

REFLECTION: FIRST GRADE

I spent a lot of time today thinking about something that happened very early on in the day with one of the boys who is probably going to be placed in a self-contained classroom. This morning he came in and was off to a great start. He was on task, quiet, and looking forward to the day. About that time the principal called and had decided that he missed too much work yesterday and would have to make it up when the class went to gym at 8:10. It was very difficult to try to explain to [the student] why he was being taken to the principal's office even though he was doing everything he was supposed to. I did not think that the consequence was close enough to the behavior to be effective and therefore was not a logical consequence. I especially thought this was a lot to ask a student for whom they are seeking an alternative placement, to understand.

Once I brought him to the office, while we waited for the principal, we started reading the story that he had missed. Again he was cooperative and on task until the principal came and took him, yelling that he misses too much work because of his behavior. I understand that at this point many of the teachers, professionals, and administrators are frustrated with him, but I think I could have worked with him to get the work done in the classroom and kept the day moving in a positive direction. Unfortunately, I was never given that opportunity and he spent most of the day in the office. I believe that each student deserves a fresh start each morning and I wish he could have gotten that today because perhaps the day would have turned out differently.

GIVING WHAT YOU WANT TO GET

Yes, this reflection from first grade is true. Your students are happier to see you each morning knowing they have a fresh start. Even if issues from the previous day still need to be addressed, and you are planning to address them, without that chance to do better and a ray of hope for forgiveness and redemption, students begin to have a fearful or negative attitude toward school—and rightfully so. This kind of discouragement can lead to anxiety, withdrawal, or increased acting out. Why would you want to be in a place where you knew you were always going to be in trouble, and where past sins counted against you?

REFLECTION: KINDERGARTEN

Today was my last day at the kindergarten. I never expected it to be this hard
to leave . . . It was so hard because I know for a lot of the children school is
the only stability they have and having another adult "leave them" is extremely
hard. I just tried to reassure them that I am going to miss them a lot and that
I needed to go to my new school to help other children like I helped them. I
handed out letters to each child that I wrote them just saying thank you for being such a great kindergartener and I am going to miss you very much, along
with two pencils. Some children would not let go of the letters. As the parents
came to pick the children up, it got even harder to leave. Parents were telling
me that their child has talked so much about me and I have really touched their
child's life, as well as some parents who worked in the classroom told me how
natural I am and they know that I am going to be such a good teacher. It took all
I had to not break down as the children walked out the door for the last time.

Greet your students at the door with a smile and a confident voice on the
first day and each day thereafter. As we said earlier, teachers are people
movers and the only way to do this kind of demanding work is by proving
yourself to be a concerned and trustworthy leader, and setting a climate that
is consistently interesting, challenging, attuned to individual needs, and that
encourages risk taking. And not to be overshadowed, the climate should also
be one where everyone accepts personal responsibility for what they do and
makes amends when they have made a mistake.

The overwhelming majority of your students want to like you and be cooperative. They really do. Be approachable and they will approach you. Have
a bad attitude, complain to other teachers about your class or particular students, get exasperated with their less-than-perfect behavior, yell at them, and
you will sour your relationships with them. You do get what you give.

By nature of their chosen profession, the heart of a teacher is big and
understanding. So whenever I heard rigid or negative attitudes expressed by
some, I wondered what prevented them from seeing life from the perspectives of others. I did all I could to break through that kind of thinking to free
their minds and hearts to feel empathy and show compassion. I did not want
to put teachers who were uncompromising or judging out into our schools to
do emotional damage to the precious children parents and society gave us in
good faith, in loco parentis.

Hopefully we now see how schools are more than just four walls filled with
a bank of knowledge to be learned, and that our beliefs and actions affect the

climate we create and, consequently, how much students learn. So, as a student teacher who is a guest in the school and the cooperating teacher's classroom, or as a beginning teacher in a new school with your own classroom, how does this understanding impact you? What can you can do to make your experience one that contributes to the positive climate of the school? How can you help build successful relationships with students, families, and colleagues? What specifically do your students need in order to be able to walk through your classroom door full of hope for what each new day together could bring? The next Essential Understanding addresses meeting students' basic needs and helps you see how to make this happen.

Essential Understanding 3

We Are All Driven by Basic Needs: Analyze Why Things Are— Or Are Not—Going Well

---

REFLECTION: SIXTH GRADE

I taught both science blocks today. The differences between the two classes are still amazing to me. I find it hard to put into words sometimes. They are just so very different. I am glad I am in the classroom more now so I can get a better sense of what each student's individual needs are, and they can get to know me and feel comfortable around me to ask for help.

The meetings and seminar I have gone to with my cooperating teacher have been beneficial, but I am happy to be back in the classroom with the students, getting to know them and what their abilities are so I can be helpful to them and to their success. I am going to be meeting with one of the aides this week or next to discuss the needs of the special needs students and go over their IEPs. We are going to go over strategies that I can use to best help them. As I wrote before, many of the students with special needs have trouble with the basics that we take for granted, such as cutting a piece of paper. I saw today how a few of them cannot take notes, and I have already started planning strategies to help them so they can be successful on the unit test coming up at the end of the month.

SEARCHING FOR ANSWERS

This student teacher expressed a sincere desire to understand so she could help each of her students. With this level of commitment we would feel assured that she strives to do what is best for her students.

I recall how strange it was to find myself in the world of school administration with no absolute answers for the never-ending stream of questions that arose. Even legal issues described in our current education law handbook had to be reviewed by the district lawyer to make sure there wasn't new case law that changed what was recently true. Every day was a challenge that required thought.

As a new teacher, you soon get used to the idea that rarely does one answer apply to most of the situations you face. It means needing to think critically about the circumstances and the people involved, and deciding what to do at this point in time. This is where your analytical skills and your belief system come into play. Part of becoming a competent teacher with longevity is to be able to deal with nuance. This requires a keen eye and ear toward the specific situation. Just as we encourage our students to figure out a new word using the context in which it is used—the words and sentences that surround it—we have to look at all the factors and nuances surrounding a given situation, and then make an educated judgment about how to respond appropriately.

We know teaching is fun and frustrating . . . to the point that you might frequently feel like giving up. Things do not always go as planned or as hoped for, so it is important to be patient and understanding with yourself, and to remember that these are children who may act differently and have varying needs from day to day, hour to hour. You probably are thinking that this is easier said than done. The answer depends on you as an individual. Keep in mind that if the students already knew everything in the curriculum and were disciplined enough and biologically inclined to be attentive and predictable no matter what, they wouldn't need to be in school. They could learn the curriculum without you. And if they always behaved predictably, in like fashion, they would be pretty boring little automatons.

People, including you and me, are just not made like that. In response to the reflection below, I asked the student teacher to identify what the students *needed* after recess and to work from that position of understanding. Together

---

REFLECTION: FIFTH GRADE

For my ELA lesson, the kids were very quiet. They seemed to be tired in the morning. I find that after lunch they are chatterboxes (I'm sure it is like that everywhere). I am not sure which strategies to use with 5th graders to get them to focus after being at recess. We have read-aloud time, which the students usually enjoy and settle down for, but today they could not stop talking. I finally said, "If you do not want to listen now, I will just read this during your free time at the end of the day." I hate saying things like that but sometimes I think that is all that will work.

we agreed they needed time to adjust their minds and bodies back to the classroom setting from the freedom and intensity of the playground, and from all the fifth-grade social drama that goes with it. They needed time to refocus, to quietly get a drink of water, and take a deep breath.

Providing them with a soothing, structured, interesting climate when they returned could help them make the adjustment. Low lighting and soft music are effective environmental manipulations that create a calmer and slower-paced atmosphere. A riddle or puzzle posted on the board provides an immediate focus of their attention. This kind of thoughtful analysis of a specific moment and situation is comparable to what you do when you analyze students' individual learning needs and respond accordingly. It is up to each teacher to approach the classroom and his students in this analytical way. It is fair and effective.

IT ALL DEPENDS

Teaching is a mix of idealism, realism, pragmatism, and faith. A wise person who is looking to effect change focuses his efforts on what he has some control over. Applied to teaching, wise professionals accept children for who they are, not what they wish they were, and then work from there. They have high expectations for their students' growth and progress toward goals, yet they view each according to needs and circumstances.

This concept of acting to ensure *equity* is based on an acknowledgment of and respect for individual differences. Treating your students equitably is not the same as treating them all equally or the same. One is fair and rational; the other is unfair, counterproductive, and ineffective. Equality calls for an exact balance, setting the same standards and approaches regardless of individual needs and expecting the same outcomes. Equity considers other factors in determining what is fair and effective for each individual. The ultimate goals may be the same, while the route may be decidedly different.

Each child and situation should be evaluated so your response is appropriate and helpful in meeting specific needs. Consider these ideas as examples of how to make equity a belief you can act on.

- Provide the student who has little adult support and few resources at home with a special homework case with pens, markers, pencils, a glue stick, and so on.
- Give the lively child who arrives in the morning ready for action a special job to do for you each day, as soon as he arrives.
- Meet privately with the child who calls out in class to jointly come up with a secret signal for you to use to remind her to raise her hand.

- Give the child who lacks the fine-motor coordination necessary to write legibly the option to use the computer to complete writing assignments.
- Situate the child who is easily distracted away from the door and the pencil sharpener.

These are specific strategies to help with specific problems, and it would be unnecessary and overly complicated to use them with every child. Teach by the principle of equity versus equality—each according to their need—and you'll make everyone's life better, including yours as a beginning teacher. With equity is the recognition that what we all know to be true in real life—that people and circumstances come in an endless variety—also applies to the students and situations in our classrooms.

The equity concept also applies to student discipline. While we have a responsibility to set clearly communicated and enforced classroom standards for behavior, we are also advised to acknowledge that each child is not at the same level of development and mastery of these social skills and attitudes. Children are at different points along the cooperation continuum and need to be met where they are. The continuum ranges from students who faithfully follow the rules and who would be emotionally scarred if disciplined sternly, to those open to learning and eager to comply, to those who push the limits periodically and are easily brought back with a look or word from the teacher, and then to the students who are so used to being in trouble they actually aim to live up to negative expectations. A stern look or quick word of refocus or correction would not likely be effective in breaking this entrenched behavior pattern. Some discipline approaches fail to recognize this principle when they aim to treat everyone the same.

REFLECTION: THIRD GRADE

What went well: A math lesson! I am getting much more comfortable with math! I had a great lesson on lines and line segments, etc., and that was followed by a review test of material I had taught over the last two weeks and all but the two most challenged students passed with flying colors! I felt great!

What to change: I had a moment when I needed to redirect a boy who was getting loud and disruptive and instead of speaking to him privately, I spoke to him in front of everyone and he tried to save face by acting like a little tough guy. It was not huge, but reminded me that I need to keep it "between the two of us" if I want to keep discipline issues calm and focused, which has been the case for the majority of the time.

MAINTAINING DIGNITY—YOURS AND THEIRS!

Take for example, a discipline program that has been around for decades originally marketed as Assertive Discipline. It is based on the flawed idea that if we make rules and consequences, and stick to them, and treat all children the same, we get uniform results. This is not true, yet the approach is still practiced in many classrooms and many new teachers either come to the classroom with an Assertive Discipline–type classroom management plan or they resort to it when they find themselves having difficulty handling their students.

Simply explained, Assertive Discipline establishes a list of rules that the class must follow and a sequence of escalating consequences for breaking the rules. A chart with these rules and consequences is strategically posted on the wall, and the teacher is the enforcer. The approach seems to confuse the classroom with a freeway, and teachers with the police. Drivers are considered adults; they are done learning and have earned the right (license) to drive. They are expected to know the traffic laws and follow them. The police are always on the lookout if they break a law. Police enforce. On the other hand, children are still learning (no license yet) and teachers teach to help them reach that goal.

The first consequence in an Assertive Discipline–type plan is a warning, where typically the offending student's name or initials are written on the board. A check mark (traffic ticket) is added next to the student's name for subsequent misbehaviors. One check might indicate no recess that day, two checks (a second ticket) might mean a note is sent home, and with three checks the child might be sent off to the principal's office (court) or, even worse, to in-school suspension (jail).

In my many years of experience, I have yet to see an Assertive Discipline management style meet its goal of sustained, across-the-board improved behavior. Rarely is a teacher able to stick to the complicated system or pleased with the outcome. The flaws are fourfold: When names are written on the board the approach does not model respect for students; it assumes every student is the same with the same behavioral issues and motivations; it sets up the teacher and students against each other, much like motorists and traffic police; and while it might get short-term compliance from some children, it fails to make long-term changes in attitudes and does not teach more appropriate behavior. While the Assertive Discipline approach has been refined to provide more privacy (name on a list instead of the board) and for their classrooms to look more caring, the legacy of the original name-on-board approach lives on in classrooms and is often a first line of defense for beginning teachers.

REFLECTION: FIFTH GRADE

The student from yesterday handled the rearranging of desks well. I pulled him aside privately and talked to him about why the desks were moved and he was contrite and the rest of the day went smoothly. At the end of the day he got a 95 on a spelling test and was very excited about it. He wanted to take the test and show it to his father, but the tests needed to stay until my teacher looked at them. I explained this to him and he was disappointed.

When the class went to their last special for the day I handed out Friday folders for each student, which contained announcements and a weekly progress report from the teacher. (Which is a great idea that I intend to steal!) I decided to add a quick note about his great grade and signed it. When he saw the note he came right over to thank me. I want him to know that even if I need to discipline him it doesn't mean that I don't care about him and his success.

This reflection identifies the balance teachers strive for between reprimanding a child and teaching the child better behavior. As you can imagine, a good deal of student teaching seminars and observation conferences for beginning teachers is devoted to how to maintain discipline, to keep students interested and attentive, to preserve your relationships with them individually, and to deal with incidents of noncompliance.

Thinking Activity: Consider This Hypothetical Scenario

In your school, faculty meetings are scheduled for every other Thursday afternoon at 3:15. The principal starts the meeting precisely at 3:15 and as latecomers walk in, he gives them a scolding look and writes their names on the whiteboard for all to see. If teachers talk to others during the meeting, they are verbally reprimanded and their names are written on the board. Please take a few minutes to think about how you and the other teachers would react to this climate. How do the reprimanded teachers feel about themselves and toward the principal at that moment? How do the other teachers feel? What has this done to their personal and professional relationships and the climate of the meeting?

Now let's consider the circumstances of the individuals whose names wound up on the whiteboard. One is a person who is chronically late to meetings and treats the meetings as a bother. Another is walking into the meeting late because he just got off the phone with an upset parent. One had a student get on the wrong bus and had to contact the parents and transportation department to make special arrangements for his pickup. One of the talkers was the art teacher, who became inspired about something the principal said, and was about to share an idea with the whole group. Another was laughing and making fun of a colleague's question. And another teacher was asking her neighbor for clarification on the date just given for standardized testing.

While the message not to be late to faculty meetings or to talk among yourselves about unrelated topics is reasonable and is being reinforced, so too is a punitive climate that fails to respect individuals, consider circumstances, and work toward solutions in private. This is not to even mention what it does to a person's dignity. Many teachers would be on edge and less apt to participate in such a climate—and even if they did not get their name on the board, they'd likely feel embarrassed for those who did and disgusted with the principal for handling the situation in this way. The unfortunate part is that such an unyielding, insensitive approach is totally unnecessary.

Apply this type of management to you and your fellow beginning teachers. An effective college supervisor or principal views each of you as an individual and fine-tunes her cognitive coaching to your strengths and weaknesses, the particulars of your placement, and the makeup of the students in your classroom. In my practice as a principal and student teaching supervisor, the first classroom observation of new teachers and our follow-up conferences provided me with valuable insight into who they were, where we needed to immediately focus our attention, and the long-term goals to set. It provided a starting point from which to work with each person as he progressed to the high quality standards of teaching we expected of all of them. The elements that were consistent were the goals; the flexibility was in how to reach those goals.

Each year presented a dramatic range of preparation, skill levels, personality traits, instincts, work ethics, and attitudes. Some students came to their field placement and first year of teaching with a commanding, confident classroom presence. Others were unsure and visibly nervous, and gave that message to their students. Some were hesitant to accept constructive criticism and to reflect on their practice. Others asked for more feedback and eagerly tried out suggestions. While one might be excited to meet the parents at open house, another was afraid of what they might ask. My job was to believe they could each eventually succeed in all these areas.

From lesson planning, knowledge of the content, classroom management strategies, and understanding of the students' developmental level, to communication skills, judgment, and instincts, my mentoring had to be tailored to their specific needs. This was done with an eye keenly focused on that ultimate list of teaching dispositions and performance standards each had to attain if they were to meet college and state expectations for certification, and the professional standards set by the school district.

Considering this dramatic range of readiness, how fair would it have been to treat all teachers the same and how effective would the experience have been for them? This would do them a personal disservice, wasting their precious classroom teaching experience. As their cognitive coach, I would be abdicating the responsibility that came with my job to facilitate their individual success. I would also be damaging our working relationship in the process, and I would probably be totally frustrated with many of them.

Does this scenario sound familiar? It is exactly what you are asked to do with the students you teach. They, too, come to the classroom with varying skill levels, attitudes, and proficiencies, which are legitimate and to be acknowledged. Treating each according to need makes educational sense and is the right thing to do. You have a responsibility to your individual students the same way supervisors have a responsibility to their individual beginning teachers. You also avoid unnecessary disappointment, hard feelings, and potential burnout.

REFLECTION: SECOND GRADE

I had the most wonderful lunch that I've ever had at this school. You showed up early, which was excellent and a wonderful surprise. I hate the atmosphere I'm in and you made today a wonderful change for me. What a way to end the week. I really feel that the conference went well between the three of us. I need to thank you for making my awful experience here much brighter. I'm so relieved that you're very understanding about my situation. Thank you, you've made my experience more bearable.

MOTIVATED TO MEET NEEDS

It is clear this student teacher was struggling. She appreciated being encouraged and recognized for her hard work and willingness to try new things. She wanted to feel like she belonged and was valued, and she wasn't getting that message.

Theories and models for human motivation are plentiful and commonly share the basic premise that behavior is motivated by needs or wants, and is influenced by circumstances and by emotional and intellectual maturity. A clear and functional explanation of what people need in order to thrive comes from the classic work *Control Theory: A New Explanation of How We Control Our Lives* by Dr. William Glasser. In chapter 2, "Our Basic Needs—The Powerful Forces That Drive Us," Glasser identifies the five basic needs that he believes motivate all behavior: the need *to belong* (to love, share, and cooperate), the need for *power* (gaining and keeping respect), the need for *freedom*, the need for *fun*, and the need *to survive* and reproduce (security).

When one or more of these needs is not being met, children *and adults* let us know by their attitudes, words, and behavior. We might not be aware that we actually *choose* our behavior depending on which basic need is or is not being met and according to what past experience has taught us about the likelihood of that need being filled.

As we know, from both our personal and professional lives, the resulting behavior isn't always pretty. Acting-out behavior by children (open disrespect for adults, truancy, bullying, vandalism, refusal to complete assignments, membership in a gang, self-mutilation, angry outbursts, throwing things, etc.) is driven by a desire to fill a need and influenced by how they have learned to best get those needs met. It may be the need to have some power in a life of chaos or abuse, more freedom in a classroom where the teacher directs all the learning, or the need to belong in a school divided into popular cliques and outcasts—and yes, this social ostracizing happens as early as the primary grades of an elementary school. The powerful drive to fill basic needs can lead children further and further from the ability to think clearly and make positive choices until they finally explode from frustration or withdraw from hopelessness.

NOT A SIGN OF WEAKNESS

A common misconception exists that if you are sensitive to students' needs and treat them each accordingly (equity), you are showing inconsistency and even personal weakness. This is an oversimplification of human motivation and the concept of equity, and it can lead to rigid, unsuccessful approaches. Being aware of and responsive to needs is actually a demonstration of confidence and power. It is evidence that the teacher has the strength to be able to step back, analyze the situation, and respond calmly and thoughtfully, as the circumstance requires. Visceral or rote responses to your students' behavior dismiss who they are as whole people and show your fear that you are not effective unless you maintain overly strict, authoritarian control. This kind of control is an illusion and usually temporary, and not only is it negative and destructive to classroom climate, it can backfire.

Children say and do things that are hurtful and inappropriate. As the professional, take a step back and do not take these outbursts personally. Even if a child calls you a nasty word, it is not necessarily directed at you as a person, but at school and the student's feelings of a lack of control. An angry reaction is likely to escalate the situation, and no one benefits from that. The student clearly has needs that are not being met somewhere in her life, and you or other students are the easy targets. Still, you should intervene to stop the behavior and deal with it thoughtfully and firmly.

Being thoughtful and understanding does not mean accepting improper and hurtful behavior and it does not mean excusing poor behavior because of a child's home life. On the contrary, it means recognizing the extenuating circumstances and being willing to put extra energy into making sure the child *learns* to make better choices, in spite of his background. It means you are willing to go beyond the superficial to get to know and work *with* the student, and to think creatively and try new approaches. It actually shows that you have resolve and personal power as you demonstrate a true, tenacious commitment to improving a student's attitude and behavior. You reaffirm your belief that she can do better, and you promise not to give up on her. This is a powerful message and it is one time that being stubborn is a virtue.

WHY DO THEY DO THAT!

At times, for various intentional and unintentional reasons, students' needs are not met—and before you know what has happened, you have a "situation." The "needs to trouble" evolution goes like this.

FROM NEEDS TO...

Child's needs not met ⇨

Frustration sets in ⇨

Lacks pro-social skills to get needs met ⇨

Chooses anger or hurtful behavior ⇨

...TROUBLE

Think about what you could do as a teacher to intervene along this progression and put a halt to the downward spiral. How might you divert unmet needs from becoming poor behavior choices? Your task is clear, though not simple: Make sure you are meeting your students' needs in the first place. This proactive approach requires consistent focus and open communication that prevents problems from arising and then escalating. The focus drives how you run your classroom and the climate you set.

How do you know what students need and when something is missing? How do you recognize when frustration is setting in and a child is giving up or getting agitated? How can you respond and intervene if the child acts out in an angry way? What actions can you take? What can you do to make sure your students have the pro-social skills to deal with life's periodic frustrations? You do all of this by being continually aware of individual and group dynamics, by communicating openly and directly, and by being a keen observer.

What the majority of children need and want from school is no different than what they need and want from their families and society. They want a place where they are valued, respected, listened to, and held to high expectations. They want to be given freedom to be responsible, opportunities to make decisions, and to share uplifting and fun times together. They want schools that feel emotionally and physically safe, with clear boundaries. As we said in Essential Understanding 2, we have a tremendous opportunity to influence our students' behavior simply by our attitudes toward them and the classroom climate we create. A positive climate goes a long way toward meeting students' needs because its policies and practices are reasonable and child-centered.

Common sense tells us to repeat successful strategies and avoid unsuccessful ones. It is a process of trying, evaluating, adjusting, and trying again. Schools that intentionally and systematically work at creating and maintaining a positive climate that acknowledges and meets basic needs at the same time reduce the negative behavior and attitudes that adversely affect a school. Unmet needs and damaged relationships prevent children from being successful students and becoming citizens of high character.

This is where genuine caring and opportunities for social interactions come into play. You are less likely to hurt, disparage, or destroy something or someone you are familiar with and care about. So students must bond with their schools, each other, and the adults they have contact with if we expect them to choose positive ways to behave inside and outside those four walls. We have to figure out what works and what doesn't. The Search Institute has a lot to offer us in this area.

ASSETS RATHER THAN DEFICITS

The Search Institute has done extensive research into the internal and external assets a child needs to develop to become a productive and responsible adult. What is so refreshing is that they approach child development with a positive frame of mind that asks: *What can we provide our students to help them mature into responsible adults?* As listed in their "40 Developmental Assets for Middle Childhood" (see Resources), these range from the *external* asset of "High expectations—Parent(s) and teachers expect the child to do his or her best at school and in other activities" to the *internal* asset of "Cultural competence—Child knows and is comfortable with people of different racial, ethnic, and cultural backgrounds and with her or his own cultural identity."

The parallel to Glasser's basic needs is clear. Our lives may be influenced by the larger society, but our needs are met through resources found in our own direct environment—home, neighborhood, school, religious institution, and local community—and ultimately by the internal strengths and competencies we develop as we mature. The belief is that if we work from an asset base (what children must have to succeed) rather than a deficit base (what children lack that keeps them from succeeding), we can intentionally provide the opportunities, relationships, skills, and support that each child requires to grow up healthy and secure.

The same works for mentoring beginning teachers such as you—we have a much better chance of being effective if we focus on and provide what you need to be a successful teacher rather than waiting to identify your deficits after you are already struggling. The Search Institute's "40 Developmental Assets" advocate this preventative approach as a proactive way to make sure basic needs are addressed when children are young, and then carefully nurtured and maintained throughout adolescence, until they reach adulthood.

Thinking Activity: How Blessed Was I Growing Up?

Go to the Internet site www.search-institute.org/assets or to the Resources section at the end of this book for a copy of the complete list of the Search Institute's list, "40 Developmental Assets for Middle Childhood." The website contains three levels—for adolescents, middle childhood, and early childhood—so choose the one you are most interested in. As you read the lists, make note of the supports you had growing up. Consider how these assets helped you to become the person you are today. Next consider the assets your students and your own children have. What, if anything, is different or has changed to raise the "asset stakes"?

—∞∞—

The nature of family structures and communities is more fragmented than that of previous generations, where extended families often lived close by and were there to support each other. Small neighborhood schools were also a means to building assets. Teachers and school communities now play an even greater role in asset building. As we address the specific role teachers have in fostering healthy academic and emotional development, the following internal and external assets stand out as areas where teachers can and still do make a difference:

40 Developmental Assets for Middle Childhood (ages 8–12)

External Assets
  Support:

5. *Caring school climate*—Relationships with teachers and peers provide a caring, encouraging environment.
6. *Parent involvement in schooling*—Parent(s) are actively involved in helping the child succeed in school.

  Empowerment:

10. *Safety*—Child feels safe at home, at school, and in his or her neighborhood.

  Boundaries and Expectations:

12. *School boundaries*—School provides clear rules and consequences.
14. *Adult role models*—Parent(s) and other adults in the child's family, as well as nonfamily adults, model positive, responsible behavior.

Internal Assets
  Commitment to Learning:

22. *Learning engagement*—Child is responsive, attentive, and actively engaged in learning at school and enjoys participating in learning activities outside of school.
24. *Bonding to school*—Child cares about teachers and other adults at school.

Now look at the assets listed under *Positive Values* and you find the language of character education: *caring, equality and social justice, integrity, honesty, responsibility,* and *healthy lifestyle.* Continue on to *Social Competencies* and you find the language of pro-social skills: *planning and decision making, interpersonal and cultural competence, resistance skills,* and *peaceful conflict resolution.* When we reach the final four *Positive Identity* assets, it is clear that a *belief in personal power and worth,* along with a *sense of purpose* and *hope for the future,* nurture the spirit of the child. These beliefs provide the strength and faith needed to keep children moving toward the adult freedoms and responsibilities that await them. Through relationships with caring adults committed to coaching, challenging, and guiding us, we believe we can succeed and are prepared with the necessary skills and competencies. We know we are loved, experience tells us we are capable, and our relationships tell us we are not alone. In his book *How Was* Your *Day at School?* Nathan Eklund wisely applies the asset approach to nurturing teachers. For more information on how assets can help teachers, please go to www.howwasyourdayatschool.org.

Isn't this what we have been talking about all along? We care about and respect those who show they care about and respect us, because such positive relationships feel good and meet our basic needs. How do we get children to love learning, believe in their abilities, and bond with their school? We do this by making sure school, thanks to supportive relationships, is a challenging safe haven. This means the beliefs and attitudes we hold about children and families are the underpinnings of our potential to be successful teachers and inspirational role models.

THINK IT THROUGH AND KEEP IT SIMPLE

Teachers and members of the school community (and supervisors of beginning teachers) should regularly ask themselves:

- What messages do the practices and policies of my classroom and school send my students?
- Are these messages in line with my beliefs?
- Are they consistent with my goals?
- Does anything need changing?

What follows is the tale of a valiant, sincere effort to bring the behavior of a class in line. Other methods were not successful and the teacher decided something more formal was needed. Some of the concepts represented in the twelve Essential Understandings are addressed: an element of control theory and basic needs; external developmental assets; and the desire to set a positive classroom climate of respect. The scenario may sound familiar.

REFLECTION: THIRD GRADE

Today I had a morning meeting with the students to talk about expectations I have. I had them tell me the rules and what they think the consequences and rewards should be. Then I told them about The Club. On the board I had written a green star with a line under it. When I caught students being good consistently their name would go under the star and they would become a member of The Club. They each had the whole day to become a member. Consistent good behavior can give them extra stars by their names, and bad behavior could get them removed from The Club. It is up to them, it is a personal decision. Before dismissal I see who is in the club. The members for the day get to put their name on a slip of paper and put it in The Club jar.

The next day The Club is looking for new members. Each day starts with a brand new slate. It's up to the students if they are in The Club or not. At the end of the week I draw out of the jar two names; those two are the Stars of the Week. They get special prizes and are my special helpers for the next week. Each day they become a member gets them more chances to become stars of the week. Everyone gets a chance. There is no limit on how many can be in The Club for the day. The students are very excited, and I've seen an improvement in behavior. They really want to become a member.

REFLECTION: THIRD GRADE, THREE DAYS LATER

Today my teacher was grading ELA tests so I had a sub in the room. The kids were more well behaved than on Tuesday. I think it's because of The Club. They have really taken to this and I have seen a noticed improvement especially in transitions. When they came in from a special or from one subject to another, I hardly had to warn them at all. They wanted to be good; they wanted me to see them being good so they could be in The Club. I have told them that I cannot watch every single child's action every second, so in order for me to notice good behavior it has to be consistent and all the time. This makes me have to discipline less, which leaves more time for games.

REFLECTION: THIRD GRADE, THE NEXT WEEK

The kids were a bit chatty today. They earned themselves a silent lunch. One thing I love about kids is that you can be stern and punish them and five seconds later they are your best friend again. . .

REFLECTION: THIRD GRADE, TWO WEEKS LATER

Today was my last day of solo teaching. It went by so fast; it will be weird
tomorrow when I don't have to teach the whole day. Again, we had a snow
day on Tuesday. We got behind a bit and the kids missed out on a special pre-
sentation and library. I also had to adjust my plans for the day when I got to
school. I've learned that I need to work on classroom management the most. I
need to develop tricks to help control the class and keep them focused during
transitions. I also need to figure out how to keep the whole class quiet when
I'm busy working with a couple of students individually and I can't keep my
eye on every single student.

These are the thoughtful, sincere, honest reflections of a well-intentioned new
teacher. She realized there was a problem, addressed it proactively, and then
found herself back at the same frustration point a few weeks later. This is the
typical and disappointing outcome of external reward systems. They start out
by offering hope and a promise of less time spent on discipline, freeing up time
to enjoy each other while learning. These systems tend to fail because the management approach does not consider what we know about basic human needs.
Everyone does not need, nor respond to, the same motivations. It illustrates how
for new teachers, one very legitimate fear—losing control of the classroom—can
overshadow all the asset-building they could be working on with their students.
They offer gimmicks when students need relationships.

Such an external reward system actually reduces a child's feeling of power,
fun, and belonging. The teacher wields the power because she has to notice the
child being consistently good for him to join The Club. Then, as soon as a student
fails to become a member of The Club or isn't randomly selected for the star of
the week, he is discouraged and no longer thinks it is fun. He is excluded and
disengaged.

It is the fear that our students will not listen to us unless we come down hard
on them that sends us searching for an artificial management system with extrinsic
motivations. Desperation, poor advice, and lack of experience managing a large
group of children often lead to a reward and punishment system to meet the need to
maintain order. Like The Club, these typically include some version of an incentive
system where the teacher posts a chart and the student gets a star or sticker next to
her name for being "good" or "helpful." The reward for accruing a certain number
of points is often getting to choose a prize from the treasure box or a special privilege. The reward could be stickers, candy, or marbles in a jar—and sometimes it
is the opposite: a punishment system where if you accrue too many checks you
lose a privilege or are punished in another way.

On paper such plans do not sound too far-fetched. We have all heard of them or seen them in action before, and might even have used them ourselves. Behaviorists and their experiments with animals tried to convince us their findings applied to people. It is more complicated than that. Such systems tempt us with their offer of a feeling of efficacy, a way to get out of the dark pit of classroom management and back to teaching. In reality these systems misread students' needs and left them unmet. They are usually too complicated and time consuming to be followed consistently and fairly, especially at the same time you are trying to teach. Consider the following scenario and how, over time, the system breaks down.

DISSECTING THE REINFORCEMENT CHART

Picture a beautifully drawn and illustrated chart, posted on the front wall of the classroom. It is the Monday after a tough few days when some students would not sit still or listen, and instead disrupted the class. The new teacher starts out hopeful and enthusiastic, posting the chart he worked on over the weekend on the front board, and explaining to the class how the reward system works: As a student is noticed for being "good," she gets a sticker next to her name. The prize is a chance to eat lunch in the classroom with the teacher. Ten stickers does it. The children are excited, too. They like a contest and would like to have the special privilege of eating lunch with the teacher. Of course they would. They like him and want his approval.

On the first day of the plan, the teacher uses the chart system often to point out "good" behavior. Good behavior is not clearly defined. As stickers mount next to certain names, some students complain that they were being good, too, but the teacher didn't see them. They say it is unfair and they deserve a sticker, too. It's time for a judgment call. The teacher may agree with the students' argument and give them a sticker or, through fear of the system collapsing and seeming weak, the teacher might inform them that the rules are the rules and complaining will not get them a sticker. At the end of the first day, the typically well-behaved students (who didn't need the artificial reward system in the first place) have amassed many stickers and the goal is within their grasp. They are looking forward to that special lunch. A few students, usually those for whom the chart is intended, have one or no stickers and are feeling let down.

In the meantime, the chart is in front of the room for all to see. It reinforces what everyone knew in the first place—who the "good" and the "problem" students are. Anyone who comes into the room gets to read it—other teachers, parents, other students, and the principal. Over the next few days the "good" students pull way ahead in the sticker race and the students who have self-control issues or other issues lag behind. They now realize they will never reach the goal. They are discouraged, and the incentive to try is gone. In fact, they have a new incentive: to cause more trouble and act like it was a "stupid chart" in the first place; they claim they don't want to eat with that mean teacher anyway! They have dropped out of what they had initially bought into.

As always happens, the time pressures of teaching mount with lessons to teach and papers to read and return, tests to administer, and unexpected assemblies . . . and now the well-intentioned teacher starts to forget to use the chart. The students who are close to the magic number remind the teacher and interest is renewed. Soon a few reach the goal and ask when they can come to the classroom for lunch. The rest of the students have forgotten about the chart and have gone back to their respective behaviors.

The chart hangs unfinished and ignored. The classroom behavior of a few students is as disruptive as it was before, maybe even worse because of their perceived failure. A few of the lucky ones eat in the classroom with the teacher and continue being cooperative in class, just as they were before.

You can see why the reward system failed—because it was cumbersome, unrealistic, and appealed to a superficial motivational level of the students. It did not teach specific appropriate behavior and classroom social and academic skills in a way that addressed the unique needs of the few students who were acting out. It did not identify and meet the needs of the students who were not completing their work. It did not help the ostracized child feel like he belongs. A reward system might work with an individual student as a short-term intervention to correct a specific, serious problem. It is not an effective long-term approach, especially for a whole class.

For a deeper exploration of the affects of stickers, praise, and grading on motivation, read Alfie Kohn's article "Punished by Rewards? A Conversation with Alfie Kohn" in *Educational Leadership*, September 1995, or his book on the topic, *Punished by Rewards: The Trouble with Gold Stars, Incentive Plans, A's, Praise, and Other Bribes.* His mega research study on motivation flies in the face of common practice.

Thinking Activity: Helping or Hindering?

Some years ago I asked the students in one of my graduate education classes to write down how we *help and hinder* meeting students' basic needs. Please try the activity yourself. Carefully consider how your school helps and hinders meeting their basic needs (we added feeling helpful). Jot down your ideas.

- Feeling cared about/belonging/connecting
- Feeling powerful/having freedom
- Feeling stimulated/having fun
- Feeling capable/successful
- Feeling helpful
- Feeling cared for/survival needs

My graduate students, many of them first- and second-year teachers, appreciated the assignment because it made them cognizant of the ramifications of their behaviors and words, specifically how they affect students and inadvertently enhance or erode the climate of the classroom. You will likely find many of your ideas in their lists that follow—they are universal concepts.

HOW WE HELP OR HINDER
MEETING STUDENTS' BASIC NEEDS

Feeling Cared About/Belonging/Connecting

We help meet this basic need when we . . . use cooperative groups, display student work, greet students when they enter the room, create a personal space for them, allow students to develop relationships, encourage student input, stage schoolwide events, offer mentors and other special relationships with caring adults.

We hinder meeting this basic need when we . . . use competition, use Assertive Discipline, use sarcasm, show favoritism, are not approachable, single students out, treat students like numbers.

Feeling Powerful/Having Freedom

We help meet this basic need when we . . . let students plan school activities, give students jobs and responsibilities, give them a say in the curriculum, use cooperative learning, use class meetings and other opportunities for students to discuss problems and ideas.

We hinder meeting this basic need when we . . . contradict or change the rules, dominate the students, put kids down, speak to them in a condescending way, do not use cooperative learning.

Feeling Stimulated/Having Fun

We help meet this basic need when we . . . use hands-on learning and group work, share ideas together, play review and other games, offer clubs, take field trips, have assemblies.

We hinder meeting this basic need when we . . . overuse worksheets, teach with boring materials, lack variety in our teaching, use a monotone voice, use a raised/scolding tone of voice, allow unstructured and hurtful recess time, use sarcasm.

Feeling Capable/Successful

We help meet this basic need when we . . . offer after-school tutoring programs, provide mentors for struggling kids, use current teaching methods, use appropriate curriculum and materials, show encouragement, teach according to each child's needs, modify instruction and tests, individualize learning, tell kids when they are successful.

We hinder meeting this basic need when we . . . lack necessary materials, put kids down, say their work is a waste, base grades on one type of assessment, do not provide appropriate assistance in the early grades.

Feeling Helpful

We help meet this basic need when we . . . give children classroom jobs, pair them up to be reading buddies, let them work with a partner, have them lead the class in activities like the morning calendar, encourage them to ask a friend for help instead of the teacher, allow them to develop the classroom goals and rules, have discussions to solve problems, use students as teacher aides in lower grades and have them tutor other children.

We hinder meeting this basic need when we . . . keep them from being actively involved in school life, do not allow them to work together, do things for them that they can do themselves, tell them everything instead of asking for their help and ideas.

Feeling Cared For/Survival Needs

We help meet this basic need when we . . . offer breakfast and lunch in school, have a class snack time, have bathrooms and drinking fountains close by, offer the confidential free and reduced lunch programs, provide before- and after-school care, house a school nurse or health clinic in the building, employ school counselors and social workers, give children a reason to attend school (such as a mentor).

We hinder meeting this basic need when we . . . punish or reward with food, create an unhealthy dependency on others, impose unreasonable time limits for eating lunch, refuse to allow children to enter the building when it is cold outside, ignore clothing or other material needs.

What I found most amazing about this exercise was that, unknowingly, my students identified all the Essential Understandings I discuss in this book! In their minds and hearts, teachers know what is right. I always knew they did. The key is to be aware of these principles and then consistently, and intentionally, *act* like you know what is right and do it.

In Essential Understanding 4, we explore positive classroom management and discipline approaches in more depth, with the focus on what you can do as a role model to meet your students' needs and avoid problems.

Essential Understanding 4

You are a Role Model:
Use Your Personal and Positional
Power to be a Positive Influence

REFLECTION: SECOND GRADE

Well, today was my last day of actual teaching, and I am not going to lie, I was sad at the end of the day. I have grown so used to teaching this class that I really do not want to stop. Once again today, J. came up to me in the middle of the day and gave me a hug and told me that he wishes his dad was just like me.

IN THE FISHBOWL

If you are a teacher, you are automatically an important role model for the students in your classroom and in the school, and for the families of the school community. Whether you want that responsibility or not, it is yours. Much of teaching happens through casual role-modeling rather than formal instruction, and it is often relegated to an unintentional dimension of classroom dynamics. Yet what we do when we are and aren't in our "teacher mode" does not go unnoticed. How we handle situations, discipline our students, speak to others, keep our word, and deal with our teaching responsibilities all contribute to what we model. Children do not miss a thing and are especially perceptive and sensitive to injustices.

REFLECTION: FIFTH GRADE

I wanted to share this reflection with you. I spoke with you about the importance of community building and trusting children to rise to high expectations. . . .One of the best activities I did today was not planned and came from the suggestions of the students. They have all missed having my cooperating teacher in the room (while I solo teach), so I suggested we do something special for her while she is gone this week. The students suggested writing her a song and I agreed, not knowing at first where we would end up. I am glad I went with their suggestion because it went so well and was a real learning experience.

   We democratically chose a tune to use as our song and started changing the words to include my cooperating teacher and our own personal touches. I think that it was such a great activity because it was student driven, tied in many of the ELA skills we have been working on, and was a great community builder. The students are already thinking about how to include the students that were not there today. They hope that K. will agree to do a small rap in the beginning and are excited to start practicing during calendar time tomorrow. It is especially nice to see how thoughtful, caring, and concerned these students are with one another because I wonder how many of them get to see that modeled in their own lives.

MODEL WHAT YOU EXPECT

Here is something to consider: Teachers are inherently predisposed to be activists. It is the basis of our job description! An activist is an "especially active, vigorous advocate of a cause" (Dictionary.com). We are vigorous advocates for the best life possible for our students. We advocate for the benefit of individuals, and for a community that finds peaceful solutions to problems, holds a compassionate view of those in need, and encourages an acceptance of differences. We want to make the world a better place, one child at a time.

   The student teacher who let the children write a song for their teacher deliberately supported them in an altruistic endeavor. She encouraged and supported their desire to do something kind for someone else. Think of it this way: If activism means being on the forefront of social justice, then activists we are!

   Each day we are presented with opportunities to show our commitment to developing schools that are safe and respectful, where all children have a chance to learn in peace. What this means is that, as activists for children, we cannot sidestep the emotionally charged issue of intolerance. We are the adults who are responsible for the safety and education of every one of our students, and our role requires us to take action when we see injustices that interfere with our goals. Whether driven by race, economic status, gender, sexual preference, or some other type of perceived division, intolerance and disrespect of those we view as different is the main cause of strife in students' lives (and in the world). Intolerance marches us up the violence continuum where the risk of teasing and rejection can escalate into bullying and physical assault.

Knowing this, school communities are obligated to actively address diversity as part of their school climate/violence-prevention efforts. The goal is to prepare teachers, parents, and students to recognize and address incidents of intolerance, and work for long-term changes in the way people think. A well-designed and well-intentioned prevention approach has an expectation of mutual respect and responds immediately and unequivocally to comments and displays of intolerance and hate. Once again, we are reminded how important it is to model what we expect. Every time we let a hurtful comment or act go by without a response, we inadvertently condone the behavior. Nowhere is your influence as a role model more clearly illustrated than in what you allow to happen on your watch.

Thinking Activity: The Dream Student—The Dream Teacher

Ask yourself: If I could design my ideal class, what would I want my students to be like? Take a few minutes to make a thoughtful list. Let's see what traits you came up with.

Did your list include qualities such as being excited to learn, kind and respectful toward others, curious about life, and hard working? These, and the others you likely thought of, are all desirable character traits for children—and adults. As a teacher, you have needs, too, and how you get those needs met dramatically affects both your experience in the classroom and the longevity of your teaching career. Good choices are easier if you remember this adage: "Be what you want your students to be." This is a variation of Mahatma Gandhi's "Be the change you want to see in the world." Most young children revere their teachers and want to please and emulate them.

It is the same with student teachers, maybe even more so, because you are a new member of an existing classroom community, a novelty, coming with fresh ideas and loads of energy. Your students learn from what you say, wear, do and don't do, and share it all at home like it is doctrine. "My teacher said . . ." is a powerful affirmation of your positional power! Showing anger and frustration, a lack of empathy, or limited awareness of diversity can hurt your students, antagonize parents, ruin your hopes for a healthy classroom climate, and undermine your career. Classroom discipline is about relationships, and a relationship where one abuses the other through positional power, age, size, or threats has no place in a classroom. You must feel deeply about children to have chosen a teaching career, and one way to show it is by using your positional power in a socially just way.

REFLECTION: FOURTH GRADE

Today I did the same science lesson I did with my class yesterday with the other fourth-grade class. This was the first chance I have had to work with the other class. I could tell right from the beginning of the lesson that the class was trying to test me. I stopped my lesson and let them know exactly what my expectations were and the consequences. I still had a couple of students testing my limits, so after the lesson I talked with them individually and let them know that I will not tolerate disrespect in my class. I am looking forward to Monday when I can see if they take me more seriously.

The fourth grade teacher above understood the importance of preserving students' dignity. By speaking with the offenders in private he modeled self-respect and respect for others. He gave his students a chance to think critically about and make better choices, skills that are essential for personal growth and maturity.

Being a positive role model reminds me of this quote from Deepak Chopra's *Seven Spiritual Laws of Success: A Practical Guide to the Fulfillment of Your Dreams*:

> Practicing the Law of Giving is actually very simple: if you want joy, give joy to others; if you want love, learn to give love; if you want attention and appreciation, learn to give attention and appreciation. . . . In fact, the easiest way to get what you want is to help others get what they want. (p. 30)

Thinking Activity: The Ones I Loved

You have already defined what you want your students to be like. Now, take a blank sheet of paper and write down the qualities and practices of your favorite schoolteachers. Think of teachers at various levels in your school career. When done, share your lists with others. What did you discover? Make a list of the universal qualities you identified and post it where you see it each day as you teach.

My memorable teachers are here with me as I write this book. They serve as positive role models to this day. I still remember Mrs. Averette and the way it felt to be in her second-grade classroom, in her presence. She was young and beautiful, a beginning teacher, and we were her first class. Mrs. Averette smiled a lot, spoke in a kind voice, let us get out of our seats and be creative. She ended each day by giving us a hug as we walked out of the building. We stood patiently in line waiting for those hugs—the girls *and* the boys. She created a magical place for everyone and I never forgot what it felt like.

Mrs. Averette knew how to treat children with respect, and she knew how to make learning exciting. She accepted each child for who he was and gave to each according to need. Her classroom was warm and safe, a lively place we treasured. We were well behaved and I don't remember her ever raising her voice. Mrs. Averette and my adored fifth-grade teacher, Miss Ostrom, had a profound influence on the kind of teacher I became. When I picture the ideal place to learn, I see back into those classrooms. I wager that a lot of my old classmates do the same. They modeled good things and we students treated them with love and respect.

Our position as teachers makes us authority figures, and this means we have responsibility for what happens in our classrooms. When something goes well or goes wrong, hold yourself accountable and determine what role you had in the outcome. Ask yourself: Did I make it or allow it to happen? Did I deal with it or excuse it? Did I reinforce it or discourage it?

Thinking Activity: The Blending of Personal and Positional Power

---

REFLECTION: FOURTH GRADE

Today we worked with number lines in my math lesson. At the beginning of the lesson a few students were still talking in their groups, so I announced that I would wait for everyone to be ready. I also reminded them that our work would be done before we get our free time in the afternoon. That worked great. As the lesson continued a few students kept talking, so I simply stopped and looked in their direction. The other students at their table told them to shhh. I definitely feel that they are seeing me more as an authority figure and they do need to listen to me. The discipline in the class is improving.

Think of groups that have positional power and how it helps them accomplish their work goals. Now consider personal power. Where does it come from and how does it affect someone's positional power? How has the positional power of teachers changed over the past fifty years? What about their personal power? Discuss your ideas with others.

—⟨⟩—

POSITIONAL POWER—PERSONAL POWER

You might have discussed how people are awarded positional power without any effort on their part; it comes with the job title or uniform. Personal power is a different story and has a dramatic effect on whether you can put your positional power to good use. It comes from your sense of efficacy, a confidence in your abilities and your mission. Confusing for teachers is the pervasive diminished respect for teachers as authority figures. In the not-so-distant past children sat in their seats, in rows, and spoke when asked. Parents would unquestioningly back the school if there were a discipline problem.

This is no longer our reality and we have to accept it. In fact we can celebrate that classrooms have become more child- and brain-friendly! What we can do is use our personal power along with our positional power to establish a balanced and nurturing classroom climate where we earn respect. Where positional power was once sufficient, we now rely on a combination of positional and personal power.

How can you accomplish this? By believing in yourself. Do not underestimate the role of personal power in your success. A police officer has the power of the uniform, a deadly weapon, and the law. Used wisely this power helps him carry out his complex job effectively and fairly, earn the trust of the community, and work with community members to prevent and solve crimes. Used unethically or with prejudice, the officer misuses his personal power, which undermines his positional power and might cost him his self-respect and the respect of others, and ultimately his career. An overblown sense of importance or power can be a corrupting force if your integrity and sense of right and wrong aren't a stronger counterforce.

The same is true of teachers and parents. They have the responsibility to use wisely and with good intentions a position of authority where they wield power over children. We know that while the majority do a pretty good job of keeping this power in check, even under challenging conditions, not everyone handles this responsibility well.

The job title gets you instant status, while your personal behavior lets you keep it and put it to good use.

You have all seen or experienced teachers who abuse their authority by demeaning, threatening, and excluding students. Their behavior is a reflection of what they think of themselves and their ability to maintain control of the classroom. This lack of a sense of personal power erodes any positional authority they once had and damages their relationship with their students. Power struggles ensue, leaving students and teachers frustrated at the acting out and waste of instructional time, and uncomfortable with the negative energy used to enforce the rules.

As a new teacher you have to know yourself well—your "buttons" and intolerances, good and bad habits, fears and insecurities—to have a realistic sense of your own personal power. Personal power allows you to teach with a calm air of confidence.

This is how you make good use of the positional power bestowed on you with your teaching degree. You *do* get what you give. The personal attitudes and beliefs you bring to teaching have a profound effect on the way the children, their families, your colleagues, and your supervisors respond to you. There is no room or justification for a negative attitude or hurtful practices. Positional power gets you into the classroom, and used well, your personal power helps you stay there. A good attitude is everything!

REFLECTION: FIRST GRADE

Today was the first day that I felt I completed all assignments and lessons in a manner that was successful. I taught six lessons, with the big ones being math and reading. Math went well for the first half of the lesson until they had to stop to go to music class. After they returned from their music class it was a little difficult trying to get them back on track, but most of the students in the class sat down and continued from where they left off in the activity with my prompting. Reading went extremely well. It was the first reading lesson that I have done and for it being the first reading lesson I took over I was happy with it.

The children seem to have a better understanding this week that I am in charge of most of the day with the exception of a few lessons. They are listening to my directions better and asking me questions during my lesson rather than my cooperating teacher. I understand that the students' level of comfort with me will take time and that their regular teacher has had these children for a half of a year and has had all of that time to build their trust. This is the first day that I left the school feeling a sense of accomplishment and success. I realize that the skills I need to learn do not happen overnight, and that they will develop with time.

WE DON'T WANT THIS TO BE YOU!

Richard Curwin and Allen Mendler have been writing about classroom discipline for years, and many still view their work on relationships between students and teachers as some of the most profound and practical guidance a new teacher could receive. In *Discipline with Dignity,* they identify a discipline and burnout cycle that begins with student misbehavior, followed by ineffective teacher responses that escalate the situation, building more tension, leading to frustration, an outburst, or to defeat (1999, p. 120). The cycle is disruptive to the classroom and devastating to the relationship. Burnout is an unfortunate result of a poor use of personal and professional resources—and the ultimate outcome is all those teachers leaving the profession.

"The guard is a prisoner, too." I once saw this on a poster and, while I cannot locate where the quote originated, I do know that the person who said it had a sophisticated understanding of power. Whoever said this realized that being in the position of control over another person or group of people is a seductive trap. It can be a corrupting force and can put you in the untenable position of keeping constant vigilance over others who have grown to resent and wish to destroy you—or at least get back at you a little. It becomes a vicious cycle of abuse of power and of defiance, of pushing and pushing back.

The teacher who lacks personal power and overcompensates with an abuse of positional power never has a moment's peace. Children have an uncanny capacity to sense and identify your insecurities and push your buttons to make your life as uncomfortable as you make theirs. Your lack of a sense of efficacy causes you to tighten up and prevents you from letting your guard down, being yourself, and connecting with your students. They, in turn, let loose as soon as your back is turned or a visitor at the door distracts you. People, especially children who are still learning self-control, take some degree of advantage of a lack of supervision. (I'm sure you've witnessed this in your own college classes or at meetings.) Relaxing is a natural reaction to a change in focus and a reduction of tension. The difference is why it is done, what is done, and how easy it is to get them back on track.

IT DOESN'T HAVE TO BE A STRUGGLE

A struggle for control doesn't have to ruin your desire to be a good teacher. You can work *with* your students instead of against them. Curwin and Mendler underscore the importance of a *responsibility model* of classroom management over the traditional *obedience model* (1999, p. 26). The obedience model sends the message that you have to follow the rules that I impose without question, regardless of your ideas of justice, special needs or circumstances, your need for freedom and power, and your temperament and personal history. You must behave in a certain way because I have positional power and I tell you to do it. Why? That old parent answer: Because I said so! But remember, when you put pressure on one place, it wells up somewhere else.

The image conjured by the word *obedience* may tempt us with its promise of order and a return to the submissive compliance of previous generations of students. This would be tempting only if we want to raise children who do not think on their own, who only behave when someone is looking, and who never question authority. Would you like the principal of your school to run the school this way? Would you want to be parented this way? The reality of this rigid and authoritarian approach is less satisfying than first imagined, and it is not very effective for today's children. It stifles that drive to question and challenge, to think critically and come to an understanding, and to make good decisions based on this process. It stifles exactly what we want informed, responsible citizens to do.

Blind obedience develops a conscience motivated by fear and an external origin of control. Not getting caught and getting even with the punisher become the motivation for behavior. If I do not care about and respect you, what you say does not matter. This drives behavior underground or causes negative energy to build up and explode. The adversarial and disrespectful environment that results damages relationships, which we have identified as the single most important factor for a safe and effective learning climate and for teacher job satisfaction.

Compare this to a different kind of message: I respect you as an individual with basic needs (*love, power, freedom, fun, survival*) and hopes, and I believe you have or can develop the skills and assets to make constructive choices. I pledge that I will guide you to personal success. Such a climate, based on rights and responsibilities, is much more satisfying and offers protection from new-teacher burnout. It gives teachers a chance to take discipline off the top of their "concerns" list.

It also leads to smart and earnest students, and eventually to citizens who have a deep sense of right and wrong, work toward the good of the community (activists!), accept responsibility for their transgressions, and understand the importance of fixing any messes they cause.

We teach students to be responsible and help them develop this internal guidance system when we ask them what they think. I am not suggesting you abdicate your positional authority. Your authority as a teacher is critically important, and it is enhanced and strengthened when you lead and coach rather than boss with rigid control. Have you ever seen a teacher angry and red-faced, yelling at a student or a class? It is not a pretty, nor a professional, sight. You damage your authority and self-respect and become a negative role model when you lose control of your emotions and say regrettable things to your students. It is weakness born of a lack of belief in your personal power and influence.

REFLECTION: SECOND GRADE

This afternoon I went into another classroom, which has children of all ages. In her room she has 3rd, 4th, and 5th grade students, all classified as special education. Wow, the structure and control in that room was very impressive. The students all showed her a great deal of respect. She was stern but fun and hands-on in her teaching and she never raised her voice and neither did her aide.

Frustration is a common and understandable feeling for teachers, and like all feelings we need to acknowledge it and respond to it in a reasonable manner. Recalling the premise that your attitude makes or breaks you as a new teacher, right from the start adopt a hopeful, optimistic approach that builds on a positive self-fulfilling prophecy. Here is a simple, quick intervention to try when you get into your classroom, one that saves *everyone's* dignity and valuable teaching time. The beauty of this approach is that you give the child the benefit of the doubt by avoiding accusations, and you save time when you redirect off-task behavior in a matter of seconds. You use your positional and personal power to help the children discover and apply the insights and solutions that already exist in their heads. All you have to do is ask them a few questions.

When the code of conduct or a rule is broken, keep calm and focus on the child's internal locus of control, and remember you are here to teach, not punish. Stay in the teacher mode and model maturity and reason. In private, calmly ask the student:

- What are you doing?
- What are you supposed to be doing?
- What do you need to do now?

This technique is simple, empowering, and effective, with no winners or losers. Then sometimes, as in the reflection that follows, you don't even have to say anything.

REFLECTION: FOURTH GRADE

I got my biggest reward as a teacher today. Many of my students came up to me as soon as they walked in the class today to tell me they showed their parents the science activity we did yesterday. They were so proud that they fooled their parents. I had no lessons today because we had the people from the nature center with us today giving presentations on animals. The kids loved it, but a few got carried away a couple times. I tried to watch them and moved around and sat with the students who were getting out of hand. My presence near them helped keep them on track.

USE YOUR POWERS TO AVOID PROBLEMS

This student teacher used proximity to refocus students' attention. Getting close to a child is much more effective that trying to make verbal or physical eye contact across the room. This holds true when students seem out of sorts. Try this simple relationship-building approach: go right up to them. If you see a child is acting out of sorts, cranky, unusually quiet, or starting fights, in private ask with sincere concern how they are. Let them know you are there if they want to talk. This violence-prevention strategy is a cornerstone of many intervention, asset-building, anger management, and classroom management programs. It works because it uses the relationships you have with your students to help anticipate and meet their needs. Caring attention may be enough to diffuse the situation, change a mood, or get a troubled child talking. Everyone wants to be listened to. It works with adults, too.

REFLECTION: SECOND GRADE

It was hard to just sit back today and not teach. The students kept coming up to me and asking questions that I could not answer. I had to send them to the teacher. All day the students kept asking me when my last day was. It was sad. All these students have different personalities and they all bring something special into the room. It was real hard to adjust at first, but I got used to them and enjoyed myself. It was a challenge, and I like to challenge myself.

One student was upset about something this morning, because she was not her usual happy self. When we were walking in the hall to go to music she was walking far behind everyone else. I stopped her and asked her if something was wrong and she said no. She would not tell me what was bothering her so I did not pry. I just told her that she could come talk to me if she needed to anytime and I gave her a hug and told her to smile. She smiled and started to cheer up. By the end of the day she was back to her normal self and I was so glad. I do not like seeing my students down like that and I try my best to cheer them up. Sometimes it works and sometimes it doesn't. This has been an amazing experience and I have learned so much from both placements. I would say I have learned more from this placement because the students were more of a challenge for me.

YOUR PHYSICAL PRESENCE

Along with positional and personal power, you also have a physical power that you convey through your body. A commanding physical power is especially evident with tall teachers, most males, and those with a loud voice and dynamic presence.

As is stressed in violence-prevention plans, when reminding or mediating watch the tone, volume, rate, and inflection of your voice. Be aware of your body language, especially personal space and hand gestures. Get down to the child's level to show your intention to work *with* the child, not to overwhelm him with your height and mass. Teachers can unintentionally intimidate if they aren't aware of their personal, professional, and physical power.

For disciplinary situations that are more serious or recurring, you can continue this problem-solving approach by using the written "Behavior Plan" included in the Resources section. It is a teaching tool that walks the child step-by-step through the thinking process and ends with him making restitution for problems he has made.

A goal of the process is recognizing that if we do something wrong we have ways to make it better. One such way is to apologize to anyone we have hurt and to try to repair any damage that was done. Give the child an opportunity and encourage him to fix his mess.

At times children can get emotionally upset and refuse to participate in a problem-solving session. You cannot force someone to calmly work through a problem if she is upset. The timing is not right for that level of introspection and you only make it worse if you push. Too many adults force children to apologize for things they have said or done. A forced apology is hollow for the giver and the recipient. An apology comes from a sincere recognition of the mistakes made and a desire to make amends. This is a thoughtful process that takes a rational, calm child. Bullying a child into making an apology is an abuse of your powers.

Teachers benefit when they are aware of the signs that a child is agitated or closing down, and know how to act appropriately. There are many excellent crisis intervention programs that teach de-escalation strategies. Read up on these and if you have the opportunity, take a training class. Every teacher should have this knowledge and these concrete skills to better handle the emotional climate of the classroom and deal with outbursts of anger and violence. After a stressful event think about what you brought and, if the answer is gasoline, what you could have done differently in that situation. If the answer is water, analyze why that helped so you can repeat strategies that work.

Staying calm and rational is a product of your temperament, self-knowledge (being aware of your buttons), training, and having the right tools and a support system with which to work. With all these pieces, you are more likely equipped to maintain control of the situation, keep people safe, and preserve relationships. Teaching is all about keeping a positive attitude, and these strategies make it less likely that you will feel the situation is hopeless or act inappropriately.

REFLECTION: PRE-KINDERGARTEN

The more I watch the afternoon group I tend to believe that a lot of their behavior issues come from what I perceive as a lack of respect. They do not respect adults, each other, or materials in the classroom. They are even destructive of toys, books, and props without remorse. Are four-year-olds capable of being respectful? I have to believe they are because most of the kids in our class seem very respectful. So, I am left wondering how to teach such young children to be respectful of people and things. I can model respect and try to explain why certain behaviors are either desirable or unacceptable. What really instills this aspect of moral development and how do you get families involved?

What deep, honest questions she posed. This was my response: "Absolutely! If taught and modeled in a consistent, firm, and caring way, they will be able to do it. You could turn them around in no time if it were your class and you could set the rules for treating people and things with respect. It is a consistent message of 'That is not okay to do' or 'Stop. We do not hurt people, throw books, etc.' Avoid over-explaining. A quick correction is better for the little ones. You could also do a mini-lesson on respect at circle time. Make it a fun thing, like a catchy song to a tune they know such as 'The Wheels on the Bus': 'The kids in the room pick up their toys . . . Our friends in the room say please and thank you . . . The readers in the room love their books . . . The people in the room are helpful and kind . . . and show respect all day!' They could act it out as they sing it. Send the words home to the families to sing with their children."

It is all about your attitude, your belief in your own efficacy, and your compassion toward your students. You *are* in charge, so look and sound like it. Go ahead and teach them better ways of being.

A caution: Make sure you do not blame the child for not knowing something or not having manners. Children come to you at all different levels of maturity and preparation. They aren't here to frustrate you; you are here to teach them. Look at yourself honestly to make sure you know the difference between acknowledging a deficit and blaming the child for having the deficit. Fight adversarial thoughts, negative attitudes, and people that pit teachers against students, teachers against teachers, and teachers against parents and administrators. Avoid toxic places in the building and stay positive and focused on your beliefs.

Teacher—your title says it all. Figure out what has to be done, make a plan, and believe you can have an impact. Choose your discipline approach through the lens of empathy, and your knowledge of child development and your individual students. Put your discipline approach through the three-question test:

- How would I feel if it were done to me or to my child?
- Is it fair and reasonable considering the age of the child?
- Does it teach my students how to make better choices?

YOU ARE THE PROFESSIONAL!

As we have been stressing, even if it sometimes feels like it, keep in mind that the children are not here to make your life difficult! *You* are here to make *their* lives better! You are the *adult*, the person with the tools and responsibility of a professional teacher. Think about your role in the dynamics of the classroom by asking yourself:

- What am *I* doing or not doing that is eliciting this negative or positive response from the child?
- What changes do *I* need to make in what I am doing to remedy these negative outcomes?
- How can *I* ensure that I continue to get these positive outcomes in the future?
- How can *I* apply these insights to other situations I face as a teacher?

Realizing you have power and the resources to make things go better can help you avoid resorting to the deadly sin of sarcasm. Children pick up on sarcasm. They might not know the word, but they feel it. There is a fine line between genuine humor and cutting remarks couched in a smile or levity. Sarcasm and other similar behaviors tell the class which child is driving you crazy.

The cues are both subtle and obvious: annoyance in the voice, repeating someone's name frequently, ignoring a child, making pointed remarks, making threats, sighing or rolling your eyes, and worst of all, singling out and embarrassing students in front of their peers. All your good intentions and training can go out the window when you are frustrated and your buttons have been pushed. When stressed we often revert to a visceral, automatic, less-than-appropriate response, and regret it afterwards.

Here is a tip. If at some point in your teaching experience you find yourself getting discouraged, make a list of something positive about each student. You might choose to share these with each child privately. This simple act can rejuvenate a relationship as it changes your attitude toward your students and sparks you and them into trying harder—for yourselves and for each other. They are honored that you care so much and have good thoughts about

---

REFLECTION: FIRST GRADE

My cooperating teacher asked me to create a list of something good about each student. She thought it would help me build more personal connections with them, and get to know each individually. I completed the list but did not realize how difficult it would be. I thought it was a great learning exercise because now I know something special about each student, and my compliments have meaning for the students and me. I am able to accent areas that they are strong in to boost their confidence in other areas.

---

them. This time the self-fulfilling prophecy is a good one. You are modeling reasonable, kind, and generous ways of treating each other, with no chance to misuse your substantial personal, positional, and physical powers.

As we will see in Essential Understanding 5, this ability to consider children as individuals helps you see how unique they and their circumstances truly are.

Everyone Has a Life Story:
Teach With Empathy and Compassion

YOU KNOW IT WHEN YOU FEEL IT

People have a natural tendency to look at others and think they have them figured out—that is, until they get to know more about the person's background and life experiences. Then they realize that nothing is as simple as it seems when it comes to people. Every person, no matter how perfect her life seems, has burdens and challenges. Every person, no matter how terrible his life seems, has joys and blessings. Once we look below the surface we realize that everyone has a story and each story is fascinating in its uniqueness and in its familiar ring. When we put this understanding to practice in our personal and professional lives, we reach a level of connectedness that allows us to see the world through the eyes of another person.

Sympathy and empathy, while both positive traits, are not the same. Sympathy is sharing the feelings of another, especially in times of sorrow and trouble. Empathy is a deeper identification with and experiencing of the feelings, thoughts, or attitudes of another person. The first is recognizing and sharing the feelings of another, while the latter is experiencing the feelings/thinking of another, as if we were that person. We give sympathy. We feel empathy.

Thinking Activity: Sympathy or Empathy?

Read the reflection that follows. Evaluate how the student teacher in this situation reacted to the events. Did he show empathy or sympathy? How do you know?

REFLECTION: SECOND GRADE

Yesterday I taught a couple of lessons that I could reflect upon, but I think I'd rather tell you about a couple of things that happened during the day. Early in the morning, at morning program, a student asked me if he could sit by his parents in the bleachers. Apparently, his sister was getting a Student of the Week award, so his parents showed up for that. I've seen kids sitting with their parents at morning program before, and my cooperating teacher wasn't there at the moment for me to ask her, so I used my judgment and said he could. I remember being a kid and the thrill of having my parents come to school, so I could see why he'd want to. Plus, he's a student that gets disciplined constantly, and he had a great day the day before (I can see that he's trying so hard to behave), so I thought it'd be a nice reward.

Well, the teacher came to morning program in the middle, and didn't say anything to me about him. When we got back to the room, I saw that he had a discipline card on his desk. I asked him why and he said it was because he sat with his mom at morning program. I can't tell you how put-off I was by this. He didn't hurt anyone by sitting with his mom. He behaved well when he was with her, and I'm sure it was a thrill for him. I can't begin to tell how badly I felt for him; especially after I told him he could sit up there. . . . I know how to manage a classroom, but I can do it in a way that no one needs to get punished for being an average second-grade child.

What did you conclude? Did the teacher employ sympathy or empathy? What served as evidence of this? How did he act on these insights? Now consider how you view students, parents, other teachers, and your administrators. Do you feel empathy toward them? How tolerant are you of their ideas and behaviors? Have you ever tried looking at a situation through their eyes? Do you catch yourself before you jump to conclusions or criticize?

MONO OR MULTI?

Our life experiences give us our personal views and perceptions. Because you believe in something does not mean it is what others believe, and we do them a disservice when we assume we know what they are thinking. One of my favorite student teaching seminars was dedicated to the concept that people are diverse in many ways—in their thinking, life experiences, aspirations, personal beliefs, and emotional triggers. To illustrate the concept, I engaged my students in this activity. It was a quiet, thought-provoking few minutes.

———ᥴᘏᔐᘎ———

Thinking Activity: Just How Alike Are We?

In private, with no discussion with anyone else, write down your answers to these fifteen questions:

1. What is your favorite kind of music?
2. Are you registered to vote? Which political party? Do you vote regularly?
3. Do you enjoy reading aloud in front of adults?
4. Where did you go to high school—in a rural, urban, or suburban area?
5. Are you a parent?
6. Should the government ensure that every American have health insurance?
7. Are your parents divorced?
8. Do you actively practice a religion? Which one?
9. What is your attitude toward amending the U.S. Constitution to ban gay marriage?
10. Do you have a learning disability? What kind?
11. What was your socioeconomic status growing up?
12. Do you believe in the death penalty?
13. Were you part of the "cool" crowd in high school?
14. Do you believe all students should have to pass the same exit exams to graduate from high school?
15. Do you support the ban on smoking in all public places?

———ᥴᘏᔐᘎ———

Afterward we shared some of the more factual questions and their responses (1, 4, and 5) and identified those that would likely cause the most heated discussions (2, 6, 8, 9, and 12). These controversial questions were the opinion questions that involved personal beliefs, cultural norms, and religious tenets. Even in this class of future teachers from the same general geographic area and racial/ethnic background, we discovered we came from diverse situations and had an array of perspectives on social and political issues.

Now consider that you are likely to teach in a public school with students and families from many backgrounds and beliefs, past experiences, and biases. Understanding that other peoples' perspectives may not align with your own is essential in all aspects of life, and it is critical in the classroom. It helps you avoid making assumptions that demean or dismiss a student's beliefs.

REFLECTION: FIRST GRADE

There were a couple of interesting things that happened on Friday. One was during calendar time. E. started crying because she believed that she had no friends because one girl chose to sit by someone else. I told her that wasn't true but she was still crying. I then asked her if she would like to write the date on the board and she got very excited and stopped crying. Then I chose one person to count the coins, or count the straws. They always need an extra helper so I asked them to choose someone and any time a helper was needed they chose E! I thought it was so amazing that they clued into the fact that she thought she had no friends and having her be the helper would make her feel better.

The other thing that happened was we just finished reading *Starring 1st Grade,* which was about a 1st grade class putting on *The Three Billy Goats Gruff,* so we made a poster inviting people to come see us. My teacher noticed that M. wrote the title backwards. All the letters were backwards and M. got very upset. I went over to her and I said that it is ok, that she can start over if she wants and I told her to come over to the mirror so her poster can do a trick. I then held the poster in front of the mirror and the letters were no longer backwards, and that made her feel a lot better. She then started a new poster, and everything was ok.

WE ARE WHAT WE EXPERIENCE

This is a beautiful example of empathy in action both on the part of the teacher and the little girl's classmates. By putting themselves in the place of the two children who were upset, the responses were compassionate and helped the students move on from their traumas.

As a teacher you work closely with parents, children, colleagues, school staff, and administrators. To develop and maintain healthy relationships, put yourself in their position. This often means stepping back and thinking before responding and acting.

Thinking Activity: Where Did This Behavior Come From?

Consider the possible reasons for these attitudes: Why might . . .

- Parents be hostile and nervous coming to a parent/teacher conference?
- A child act out whenever it is time for math?
- The custodian grumble when you've done a glitter project?
- Your principal appear irritated when you walk in just as the morning bell rings?
- A colleague seem standoffish when you come up with a creative idea?

Just reading these questions jolts us into realizing how complicated people are. As a teacher your primary responsibility is to get to know and care for your students as best you can. Students have many reasons for outbursts and for acting defiantly or putting little effort into their work. It is largely dependent on how well they are prepared for the rigors of school life. When working with your students, consider the resources and stressors each brings to school, such as level of family support, learning needs, or health conditions that interfere with his ability to learn. If we want to serve a student well, we think about her socioeconomic status and prior school history, what her family life is like, how she views herself as a learner, and how she fits in socially. We think about her story.

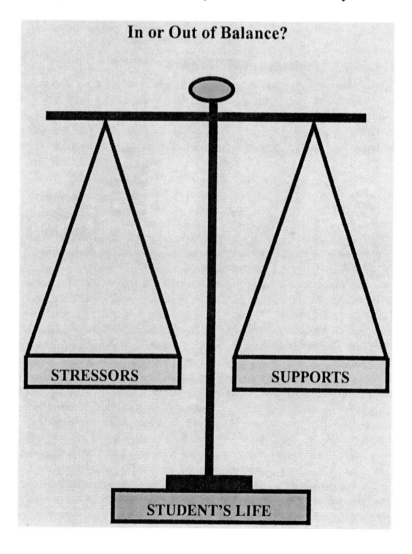

Thinking Activity: In or Out of Balance?

Choose a child you know or have worked with in your classroom and consider his resources. List stressors and supports on the appropriate side of the resources balance scale. Consider how this knowledge could help you work effectively with this child.

What types of resources did you identify? Which ones were missing? How did these relate to the Search Institute's "40 Developmental Assets" discussed earlier? How did this information affect your view of this child and what might you do differently as a result?

REFLECTION: FIFTH GRADE

The day went well, until the last science class at the end of the day. I let the students study for 10 minutes before taking the quiz and ask any questions they had. The classes used this time to study, but I ran into trouble the last class. A girl asked me if they did badly if they could retake the test. I told her that if a lot of students did badly then that would mean there was something wrong with the test or my teaching so I would let them, but if only a few people did, then no. So I handed out the quizzes. ten minutes or so later she turned in her test and sat at her seat. Then in another 10 minutes someone came in and said her mother was here to pick her up, and I said bye and have a nice four-day weekend. She turned to me, gave me a nasty look, and then turned away and stormed out of the classroom.

I was so shocked; I didn't know what to do. I figured I had made her upset by saying she couldn't retake the quiz, but I can't tell them that they can retake a quiz before taking it because then they wouldn't try on it. The teacher was not in the room at that time because she was running errands, so when I filled her in on what happened she told me that the girl has OCD (Obsessive-Compulsive Disorder), and that it wasn't my fault. My cooperating teacher (CT) said that she gets like that, and has mood swings, and whenever she has to take a quiz or test she gets upset.

I still feel badly though because I feel like I could have handled her in a better way when she asked the question. But I couldn't tell her that they could retake the test because they would walk all over me and not try the first time. My CT told me that there are other things going on as well and that I didn't do anything wrong.

I just feel like maybe next time I give a quiz or test I will take her aside and tell her not to get stressed, and that if she feels she is getting too frustrated with it then she can go out in the hall for a minute to relax and then come back in and finish it. When I was grading the tests later I noticed that she had answered only 3 out of the 15 questions. She had just given up. Tuesday (we don't have school Monday) I am going to go talk to her and make sure everything is all right. I'll tell her I'll give her another chance on this test, but next time she needs to talk to me first if she feels she is not ready for the test and I can help her so she is not so upset about it.

THE POWER OF INFORMATION

Information is another type of power to add to your personal, positional, and physical powers. It was unfortunate that this student teacher was not made aware of this particular child's special needs beforehand. She then could have used the information to anticipate problems and to respond with logic and empathy. By her response we can tell that she is a compassionate person and would go out of her way to do what was best for her students.

Perceptive teachers take time to gather information about other people so they can put the behavior, attitudes, and fears of those they work with in context, and approach them from a position of understanding. Much more gets done and much grief is avoided by looking at things from the other person's perspective. It enhances your personal power because others appreciate your reasonableness. You can be more successful working as a team when you are seen as approachable and fair.

Successful encounters and problem solving requires that you know where people are coming from. Applying empathy to your role as a teacher works like this.

Create this mental image:

- Visualize yourself as the other person—student, parent, coworker, principal.
- Look back at yourself and the situation to see things through their eyes.
- Now come back over to your side and look at the other person.
- Use what you have learned about that person to thoughtfully choose your approach and words.

Thinking Activity: You Didn't Do Your Homework? Again?

Take a few minutes to brainstorm reasons why a student may fail to complete and turn in homework. Once you have identified the possible barriers, brainstorm the constructive things you could do to turn this situation around. Consider the critical factor of family involvement and ways you could recruit the student's family as a partner without putting the problem on them to fix.

This isn't an exercise in finding excuses. It is an exercise in understanding cause and effect, and changing negative behavior patterns. Understanding is not the same as condoning or excusing. It is a strategy where you gather and use all the information you can find to help solve a problem. It is logical, considerate, and practical.

REFLECTION: SECOND GRADE

My class is creating a banner for the Walk/Run to raise money against drinking and driving. A local dairy is sponsoring it so we came up with an idea to have a person sitting at a drink counter and asking, "Got milk?" We are going to have soda, juice, Gatorade, and other non-alcoholic drinks on the drink menu at the counter.

The children are real excited about doing this. I am so glad that they are finally getting interested in something for school. One student made a comment that he did not want to do this "stupid poster." I was so proud of this other student in the class because she then said that it was not a stupid poster, that it was for a very good cause and that they should be excited just because they are helping save lives. I could not believe she said that. It was so amazing, especially because it came from a student who does not have the nicest personality.

This made me realize that we have to look past their attitudes and see what is deep inside them. Most of them probably have their attitudes because of the home they live in and they might need these attitudes to survive on the street. I see these students' attitudes as a shield they put up and I am starting to break them down by joking around with them a little and being my caring self. I am excited to work on this banner with them and cannot wait to see how it turns out.

I love this reflection; the pure joy and optimism it conveys is contagious. The student teacher had a spontaneous moment of revelation that changed her beliefs about children. This was a powerful moment in her young teaching career.

Another student teacher told me she found sitting through parent conferences to be unsettling. She felt the teacher could have done more to help an already distraught parent feel more hopeful about her child's potential to improve. This student teacher was a parent and could put herself in the mother's shoes. She made a promise to herself that when she had her own class to always find positive things to say about a child, to be kind and considerate of parents, and work with them as a team.

Going back to the previous discussion of models of discipline, we see how empathy and compassion have a role in effective classroom management. No matter what, be thoughtful and reasonable, consistent on follow-through, and give students feedback on their progress. This ability to have empathy and compassion also helps us form a healthy partnership with parents.

·⊱✦⊰·

Thinking Activity: How Are Your Students Unique?

For Essential Understanding 4 you made a list of one positive observation about each child. Now expand the list with the many ways they are unique. The more you can articulate these special qualities, the better you can celebrate who they are and address their needs as you prepare for and teach them.

·⊱✦⊰·

This works for classes and groups as well. For example, you teach two sections of the same class. You have discovered that the morning class responds well to step-by-step directions written on the board. They also benefit from having the first few problems modeled for them, doing a couple on their own, and then coming back as a whole class to check for understanding. Then they are ready to work independently or with a partner. The afternoon class as a whole you find to be more independent, and students are able to process oral directions well. After one practice example, they can complete the rest on their own or with a partner. They are quickly ready to apply the concept to new situations. It makes good educational sense to treat them differently.

As you actively focus on making your classroom a place for everyone to thrive, remember that everyone has a story, even you! This allows the kind of tailoring that makes both students and teachers less frustrated. What in *your* story would help people better understand you and your perspectives? Now find that story in each of your students. As we will see in Essential Understanding 6, parents also have a story worth hearing.

Parents and Guardians Are Your Allies: Capitalize on This Valuable Asset

BOUND BY SHARED RESPONSIBILITY

No doubt about it: You need parents and they need you, and your students need both of you. If you work confidently from a position of personal and professional power and empathy, with the belief that parents love their children and want to do what is best for them, you will discover the power of a strong parent-teacher partnership. Initiate and nurture these partnerships. In one school, parents may be actively engaged in everyday school life as classroom and school volunteers, bus monitors, or tutors, while in another they may serve as room parents for parties and nothing else. You have influence over the way parents are included and treated in your school.

REFLECTION: SECOND GRADE

Today was parent-teacher conferences, and to my surprise all of the scheduled parents showed up. I was pleased with how the conferences turned out. I was able to talk a little with each parent about their child, saying just small things that I've seen that my teacher didn't mention. I was surprised at how receptive the parents were to my comments. I thought that they would just kind of blow them off due to the fact that I am simply the student teacher, but they were very receptive and appreciated the feedback that I gave them.

The two parents that I really wanted to talk to were there today so I was happy over that as well. Those two parents were the parents of students who sit at table five. I was able to tell them about the type of behavior that I see, and the types of behavioral expectations that I have for the entire class. I also told the parents about the changes in the discipline system that I have made this past week.

FORMING A RELATIONSHIP

REFLECTION: SECOND GRADE

Thursday was a very long day. It was open house night. The students have been working all week to prepare things for open house. I was nervous to go to the open house to meet the parents. It was nice to be able to see the children with their families. Some of the parents aren't what I would have expected. Out of our 17 students only four didn't come to the open house. My cooperating teacher introduced me to all the parents. I spoke with almost all of them. They actually seemed more interested in asking me questions about my schooling and where I was from than questioning me about their children. I had expected to be questioned about their kids. It was fun though. The kids are different when they're around their families.

Open house, calling home about a problem, getting a phone call from a parent, parent-teacher conferences, the chance meeting in the hall . . . most student and beginning teachers are unprepared and a bit apprehensive to do this sensitive work with parents, and some veteran teachers may never get to the point where they welcome such interactions. This is to be expected with new teachers when you consider they have not yet had the opportunity to work closely with parents and to build their confidence. We cannot easily forget those tales we hear about demanding, defensive, uninvolved, and sometimes aggressive parents. This preconceived notion sets the stage for a "them against us" attitude.

I experienced this trepidation myself one September when I joined a new school and was quickly warned that I had a difficult parent in my classroom. I was told she would want to know everything that was going on and would be at my classroom door all the time. This warning, while well intentioned, turned out to be unnecessary and destructive. Before I had even met this mother, I viewed her as a potential problem and my attitude was to protect myself when I interacted with her. This was against my nature and affected my interactions with her and her son—but only for a short time.

It wasn't long before I regained my perspective and the confidence that I must and could work with anyone. I mentally started over with her. Our relationship grew as it was meant to grow and I found that with me she was none of the things I had been warned about, which were more likely the product of a personality conflict than innate bothersome behavior. I interpreted her actions and motives in a very different way and understood her perspective: As a young single parent she was insecure in her parenting and hadn't grown to trust putting her child in the hands of a school system. She wanted what was best for him, and for his teachers to recognize his special qualities.

We quickly developed an excellent working relationship that benefited her wonderful son. By the end of the year I viewed her as a friend, and we stayed in touch after they moved from the district. It all depended on *my* attitude, not someone else's ability to use empathy to understand and accept. Only I could determine the form our relationship would take, and I never made that mistake again. My relationships with parents and guardians were of my own making and were a cherished aspect of my life as a teacher and principal.

THE FACE TO FACE

One of my student teachers told me about a parent conference she attended with her cooperating teacher that shed light on a student's home situation. She expressed how talking with the mother helped her have empathy for the student and his struggling parent. The boy lived with his terminally ill grandmother, a little sister whom he often took care of, and a mother who worked third shift (midnight to 7 a.m.). And his father was in prison. My student teacher described the conference as heartbreaking, and it was clear that she was going to keep his life story in mind as she worked with him. Through information shared by a parent she had learned the value of communicating and understanding rather than assuming and judging.

Thinking Activity: Parent Conference Viewpoints

For this activity, use the "It's Parent Conference Time" chart to take on the role of either the *student*, the *teacher*, or the *parent* involved in a parent-teacher conference. From the perspective of a person in your role, write down your ideas for the best conference (*wildest dreams*) and the worst conference (*worst nightmare*) you can imagine. Repeat the process with the other roles. If you are working with a group, have each person focus on just one perspective.

Compare the three perspectives. What did you discover? What was it like putting yourself in someone else's place? My guess is that it wasn't too much of a leap to do this. We are full of insights yet to be tapped.

To complete this activity, use what you just learned about perspective being the lens through which a person sees a situation and jot down ways you, as a teacher, could increase the likelihood of a productive parent-teacher conference for everyone involved.

It's Parent Conference Time!

Your Wildest Dreams	Your Worst Nightmares

One of the challenges you may have identified is how to best handle the situation of divorced or separated parents and shared custody. The first thing to remember is to not take sides or encourage either parent to speak ill of the other. You are a neutral party except when it comes to the welfare of the child, where you serve as the activist advocate. If the parents choose not to attend the conference together, which is common, accommodate them by scheduling two conferences, sending report cards and notices to both parents, and so on. Your efforts go a long way toward establishing trust with the parents and providing a safe climate in which the child is not caught in the middle.

Also, think about how it feels to parents who are divorced or separated, or who never married, and to their children to be referred to as "broken families." It may be a commonly used term but it isn't very accurate and certainly is not positive. Its negative connotation implies dysfunction and evokes pity.

It is kinder and more respectful to simply state the relationship: The child's parents are divorced; she is a single mother; he is the child's stepfather; they are the foster parents. Again we see the value of teacher attitudes and behaviors that avoid summing up people by assigning them a label. Labels take the humanity out of your view of the person and force them, like a peg, into a certain hole—easy to sum up, easy to misread, and easy to dismiss.

THE PATH TO A PARTNERSHIP

How do we move from *respect* to a deeper relationship of *trust* with parents and guardians? First you have to care enough about the relationship to try.

The progression goes like this:

Respect: I value you as a person.
  Empathy:I feel what you feel; I can walk in your shoes.
    Compassion: I think and act in ways that show I understand and care.
      Trust: Earned with respect, empathy, and compassion over time.

From respect to empathy to compassion to trust. Successful parent-teacher interactions, formal and informal, require that ability to be empathetic, to put yourself in their place and use that information to everyone's advantage. Here is a chance to practice that skill.

Thinking Activity: Oh, No! There's a Problem at School!

Katie is in trouble at school. As you did with the parent conference activity, look at the same event through the eyes of the three major players in the situation—Katie, her teacher, and her parents.

- You are Katie's teacher. What is going through your mind when you place the call to Katie's parents?
- You are Katie's parent. What is going through your mind when you get the call from Katie's teacher?
- You are Katie. What is going through your mind when your teacher tells you she'll be calling your parents and when the phone rings?

What did you learn from looking at an experience from the perspective of each participant? How would this impact your choice of behavior as you work to solve the problem? Share your ideas with others and tuck this exercise in the back of your mind for when you face—and you will—this type of situation.

The previous thinking activities show us that fear is a major impediment to developing relationships. Imagine what it is like for a parent to get dressed for a meeting at school, to go into the building, check in at the office, walk down the hall, wait until it is time to go in, walk into the classroom, sit down across from the teacher, and then listen to what the teacher has to say about the child. Many things could be going through the parent's mind and through your mind to make you both nervous. This would be less of a stressful meeting if you already had had a few positive interactions with the parent. Friendly interactions and communications help you and the parent get familiar with each other to reduce those fears.

THE GOOD BEFORE THE BAD

From the beginning of your assignment as a teacher, it is helpful to have a variety of ongoing *positive* communications with parents. Some ways to do this are:

- Make home visits or send postcards/letters before school starts.
- Use a system of student agenda books that are sent home daily and include a place for parent and teacher to communicate with each other.
- Provide each child with a home/school folder for notices, personal notes, absence forms, and so on.
- Write a class newsletter or *Friday Note* to send home.
- Host a mini open house for your classroom or grade level a couple of times during the year.
- Use parents as classroom volunteers to help with projects, read with students, and chaperone field trips.
- Invite parents to visit the classroom for small performances such as dramatic presentations of a story or an authors' tea.
- Welcome parents to parent-teacher conferences by putting chairs and a desk outside the classroom where they wait.
- Include some books and school projects for them to look at while they are waiting, and maybe a bowl of hard candy for a dry, nervous mouth. (Works for you, too!)
- Design homework assignments that involve the parents in a fun, meaningful way.
- And one of my favorites: the good news contact—make random phone calls and send notes home that celebrate the child's successes or just show appreciation for who they are.

This foundation of positive experiences serves you well when you have to contact a parent about unpleasant situations and field her calls when she is unhappy. As the teacher (the professional in the relationship), you can do a lot to make those kinds of phone calls successful. You may even be asked, as were some of my students, to do this during your student teaching experience. Before you get to this point it is important to keep your supervisors and principal aware of any brewing concerns and to confer with them before contacting a parent.

Since teachers are responsible for keeping parents informed about their children's progress, successes, and transgressions, you should be highly skilled at communicating. The trick is to use your positional and personal power wisely through the lens of empathy and compassion. Remember that the goal is to establish a foundation of trust to create a working partnership with the parents, which ultimately benefits the student. Go into the situation with the frame of mind and self-confidence that something good will come of your efforts. Being prepared boosts self-confidence, so take time to prepare for the call. You can be more relaxed and communicate more effectively if you know what you want to say and how to say it in a straightforward way. You are also better situated to actively listen to the parent. Keep in mind that you are talking about an emotional issue—the welfare of his child.

Preparing for the Call

- Lay the foundation. Make sure you have had some of the positive contacts mentioned before you have to make a call home about a problem.
- Wait until you are calmed down to call.
- Choose your words carefully; use non-labeling words that *describe* the situation.
- Rehearse what you want to say.
- Make a reference sheet of the facts and points you want to make.
- Keep in mind that if the problem happened at school, the school has the responsibility to solve it, not the parent; you are looking for assistance.
- Remember that you are trying to get the parents to work *with you* to find a solution.

Initiating the Call

- Have a paper and pen to take notes.
- Put yourself in the parent's place.
- Be friendly, polite, and professional and begin the call on a congenial note.

- Address parents by their correct name (check the records first).
- Convey that you want to help, through your choice of words and tone of voice.
- Avoid putting the parent on the defensive or telling him to take care of the problem.
- Share your genuine concern for the child and your desire to work toward a solution.
- Remain professional and positive.

Discussing the Problem

- Let the parent talk and listen carefully to what he says, both in words and between the lines.
- Take notes during the conversation.
- Calmly explain the situation and/or have the child explain it.
- Put a realistic, yet encouraging, spin on being able to solve the problem.
- React calmly to the parent if he is upset; keep in control of your own emotions and responses.
- Assure the parent that you know it is not easy for him to hear that his child has a problem.
- If you are also a parent, tell the parent that it would be hard for you to hear this kind of news, too.
- Ask the parent if he has any thoughts about what happened.
- Listen to him and remain understanding of his perspective.
- Share your perspective.
- Remain professional and positive.

Finding a Solution

- Offer and solicit suggestions; take notes.
- Ask about things that work at home.
- Decide together what the consequence/approach is.
- Discourage harsh or nonproductive ideas.
- Make a set time to check back with each other to see how the plan is working.
- Ask the parent if he has any questions.
- Thank him for his support of the plan and for working with you.
- Remain professional and positive.

Concluding the Contact

- Invite the parent to come in to talk if he would like. Include the student in the discussion.
- Meet with the child to explain how you and her parents are working together to help her make better choices.
- Send a note home that summarizes the problem and the solution, and thanks the parents for their help (run it by your cooperating teacher, mentor, or principal first).
- Sign and date it, and keep a copy for yourself.
- Implement the plan and do what you can to help the child be successful.
- Contact the parents at the agreed-upon time.
- Remain professional and positive.

COMMON SENSE

Parents love their children, and so do we; they have a profound responsibility, and so do we; they know a lot about what makes their child tick, and so do we; they want a bright future for their child, and so do we. It is just plain natural that we should work together. The bright futures we wish for our children come to those who have internalized what it means to be a good person. Essential Understanding 7 explores the connection between what we do in our classrooms and the caliber of adults we present to the world.

Essential Understanding 7

Character Education, Violence Prevention, and Multiculturalism Are not Separate *Programs*: Make Them an Integral Part of Your Everyday Teaching

It is an ongoing challenge promoting a philosophy rather than a program.

—Colleen Mahoney (in Starkman et al., 2006, p. 86)

I agree. A *philosophy*, like a belief system, develops through personal effort and introspection. It is "a system of principles for guidance in practical affairs" (Dictionary.com). A *program* is "a plan of action to accomplish a specified end" (Dictionary.com). A commercial program has already been pre-thought-out and organized by someone else. A philosophy is overarching and a pervasive component of your life. A program is a set of materials and activities, implemented for a period of time to accomplish a specific outcome. Big issues like multiculturalism, violence prevention, and character education deserve to be part of a philosophy that drives your choices in life.

A WAY OF LIVING AND TEACHING

Look around you and you see that diversity abounds. The goal of multicultural education is to prepare students to be successful in this diverse world. It is the practice of acknowledging and respecting the differences of thought, spirituality, customs, foods, dress, and mores that naturally come from various cultures, religions, races, ethnicities, and opinions within a community. Multicultural education creates familiarity by infusing different cultures and perspectives into all aspects of the curriculum and school life. It strives to teach students to consider different perspectives in evaluating historical events, current events, and everyday happenings.

In our classrooms it also comes from more subtle distinctions such as socioeconomic status, learning disabilities, where you live, athletic ability, family makeup, cliques and clubs, and how you look. Adults have the responsibility to take a proactive stance by setting an expectation of respect for these differences, and by responding immediately and unequivocally to comments and displays of intolerance.

Starkman, Scales, and Roberts, writing for the Search Institute, said it eloquently: "Developing assets is certainly about 'doing' but it is also about 'being.' Asset building is not another thing to 'do.' When you implement the asset framework, you don't just add programs to an already overloaded curriculum, and you don't just add tasks to the schedule of already overworked school adults. You infuse whatever else is happening with a way of being, a philosophy, a lens with which to view the learning and development of students" (2006, p. 105).

LIVING BY A CODE—ALL OF US

We all must have a code to live by that reflects our beliefs and gives us guidelines for our behavior. Life would be confusing and overwhelming if we had nothing on which to base our choices. Many successful teachers are driven by the belief that people are more likely to follow, and see as fair, guidelines for behavior (rules) they have explored, understand, and have a role in developing. This is in contrast to the imposition of rules and consequences of some discipline approaches. The school, classroom, and home are natural places to give children an active role in defining their code of conduct—what is and isn't okay. This includes defining what it means to be part of a healthy, well-functioning community. Make sure your students know what you expect from them and help them define what they expect from you and each other. As you share your power with them, you give them personal power, one of the five basic needs.

One project in particular stands out from my time as an elementary school principal at Maine Memorial Elementary School in upstate New York. As a school community, we developed a schoolwide code of conduct. During the first week of school, every teacher worked with his students, in kindergarten through fifth grade, to define what it took to be a positive member of the school community. The teachers in each grade level then collected all the class charts and worked together to synthesize the concepts. Finally, the grade-level team leaders brought their charts to a vertical team meeting (K to fifth-grade teachers) where they were again synthesized into a few statements of principles that covered the ideas expressed by each grade level. The result was a large chart stating the Maine Memorial School Code of Conduct.

Next we held a schoolwide assembly to share the results of our joint efforts. With some fanfare we revealed the code to the students. (We actually did an unveiling!) We read it together and had the students identify the ideas they recognized from their own classroom discussions. The code was a clear expression of what will enable us to live and learn together in peace. It was easy enough for the kindergartners to understand and sophisticated enough to challenge the fifth-graders to think conceptually. This simple and powerful code was printed up on large pieces of paper and then posted in each classroom and throughout the building, including in my office, where it served as a starting point for discussions about behavior issues. We also sent it home to families so they could share in and reinforce the principles.

Here is what we all came up with for our schoolwide code of conduct:

> We come to school to learn about our world.
> We are responsible for:
>
> - Our choices, our learning, and our environment
> - Treating others with kindness and respect
> - Helping and sharing
> - Working together
>
> We look out for each other!

It would have been easier to just compose the code myself and hand it out to the students and teachers, but that would not fit with my beliefs. By creating our code together we all had a stake in seeing it followed. By sharing in my power, the students grew in their sense of efficacy. Each time you choose to do something like this it is a positive learning experience for others.

When you are a student teacher, unlike a newly hired teacher with her own classroom, you inherit and have to find a way to work within your cooperating teacher's management style. If a code of conduct does not already exist, discuss with your cooperating teacher the idea of leading your students through a classroom version of this process. This is a dramatic and effective way to establish that you are now the teacher in charge, that you believe in the students' ability to make good choices, and that you are going to work *with* them to uphold the code of conduct. Your message is clear—while you may be learning how to teach, you know what you expect from them, and you are here to help them succeed. You have defined your authority and thoughtfully avoided putting yourself into a power play with your students.

REFLECTION: SECOND GRADE

Today was a better day. The students were better behaved and I was impressed with their ability to work together today. There were only a couple of arguments amongst them, but nothing too serious that it took a while to calm them down. They even painted their baskets and did not fool around with the paint. I was so surprised and impressed with them. They shared the paint and did not fight over the different colors. They took turns and I even saw a couple of students help each other with their baskets. It was a good day compared to the other days I had this week. The students are even starting to talk to me more and open up. I started to get worried because they would not talk to me. I am slowly gaining their trust though. I talked to my cooperating teacher and asked him if it would be all right if I had a talk with the class after break about what it looks and sounds like to be respectful and how to work with a partner or in groups. He said that would be good.

IT TAKES VIGILANCE

Thinking back to Essential Understanding 1 where we identified student safety as our number one priority, it makes sense that teachers need to be consistently mindful of issues of tolerance and respect. It is important that these attitudes are reinforced in all of our rooms and throughout the school. This is actually easier than it might sound and is more effective than delivering separate programs that heighten awareness and then end, only to be followed by the next mandate.

The more effective way is a combination of the two approaches: exposing students to awareness-raising instruction and activities, and supporting these concepts and skills with routine curricular and social expectations. In the same way that personal beliefs become second nature and guide the way *we* teach, these expectations of cultural understanding and respectful behavior toward all become second nature to you and your students. Nothing is more satisfying than hearing a child say things like "We don't hit in our room" or "I'm sorry I said that." It shows she has internalized the principles and is on her way to making them part of her character. Many character education efforts become scripted, lock-step programs that have a start date and an end date, and never seem to make it to their rightful place, deep down in the soul of all members of the school community.

Bullying is a serious form of violence and is a significant cause of student anxiety. It is a roadblock to learning and a cause of truancy. How can teachers keep students safe from the bullying that is pervasive in our schools, especially during unstructured times in the classroom, on the school bus, and at recess?

This bullying can take many forms, from typical male aggression of verbal taunts, angry outbursts, extortion, and physical fights, to the less obvious female relational bullying that uses isolation, exclusion, rumors, and withholding friendship to hurt others. They are both devastating to individual children and the climate of the school. Keep in mind that, unlike the arguments boys tend to get into and quickly recoup from, the kind of bullying girls use to exclude others lingers on and continues to do emotional damage. An excellent book on the subject is *Odd Girl Out: The Hidden Culture of Aggression in Girls* by Rachel Simmons.

Not long ago a neighboring community witnessed the ultimate display of intolerance expressed as a shocking act of violence. An openly gay middle school student sitting in the school's computer lab was shot by a classmate who, it was reported, was intolerant of his sexual orientation. The disturbing case made national news and magazines, and was the subject of an article in *Teaching Tolerance* magazine. The child died and once again, parents, community members, and the students called on schools (teachers and administrators) to keep a closer ear to the undercurrent of bullying and intimidation we all know exists. Communities want schools to be more proactive. The most effective bullying prevention programs are those where it is everyone's responsibility—parents, students, staff, faculty, and bus drivers—to monitor, report and intervene as soon as such behavior is suspected or exhibited. This is a prudent mandate, and teachers and administrators do have a primary responsibility, as they serve in loco parentis and have the opportunity and power to keep schools safe.

MODEL, TEACH, MODEL, REMIND, MODEL, REINFORCE, MODEL, INTERVENE

Teachers have a profound ability to affect students' attitudes by making the development of pro-social attitudes and skills an everyday priority. Below are some things you can do to set an expectation of nonviolence that reduces aggression and prevents bullying in your school.

- Model calm, fair, just behavior every day.
- Evaluate yourself for bullying-type behavior (sarcasm, verbal ridicule, yelling, standing over a child, pointing a finger in a child's face, unreasonable punishments, favoritism, etc.).
- Work *with* the students to establish clear rules about appropriate behavior.
- Tell students to come to you if they are being bullied or know someone else is being bullied.
- Discuss the difference between tattling and reporting bullying or threats.

- Know what the school's policy is and together with your students, make a classroom mission statement (e.g., "We treat each other with respect and kindness and help out whenever we can").
- Become more educated about bullying; know what to look for and be more aware of body language.
- Learn about the more subtle relational aggression girls use to bully and reject others.
- Role-play the three roles in a bullying situation: the bully, the victim, and the audience/observer; have the students apply the roles to school incidents and to current local and world events.
- Provide examples of situations and discuss options for reducing both the obvious verbal and physical bullying and the less overt rumor spreading, exclusion from playground clubs, and e-mail attacks.
- Pay close attention to students, watch what is going on, and intervene immediately.
- Do not downplay or ignore incidents or what a student tells you.
- Integrate related lessons and discussions into the curriculum.
- Learn conflict resolution strategies and teach them to your students.
- Establish open communication with students so they feel safe coming to you with a problem.
- Share your efforts with families so they can do their part.

REFLECTION: FIRST GRADE

I decided today that this class is in dire need of class meetings with character education. People are constantly hitting each other, telling on one another, and complaining when they have to work with certain partners. I'm going to ask my cooperating teacher if it is okay for me to incorporate this into my morning circle time.

I know that this class can behave and work together, they just need to be directed how to do it. I realize that many of these students aren't getting what they need at home to be able to contribute positively to the classroom society.

I'm tired of the constant tattling every time this one particular girl moves an inch. She gets yelled at a lot and the other kids know it, and then they tell on her every chance they get. The poor girl can't even play with a tiny piece of paper she found on the floor without being told on. This girl also wet herself twice today, and there might be a correlation here. I mentioned that there needs to be some extra outside help by a social worker and a psychologist because she is a smart girl but something just isn't right. Plus the teacher hasn't even seen her parents once this year.

- Inform your supervisors and principal if you suspect someone is being bullied.
- Remember that, in a school, every student is your student . . . in loco parentis.

This young girl was in obvious need of help. A climate where she was the victim and the other children the bullies, with the adults as unaware or passive bystanders, is unconscionable and could only exacerbate her problems. You can do so much to teach compassion and acceptance by building familiarity among students. Through a matter-of-fact expectation children get used to working with each other. Arrange situations where children work with other students with whom they usually do not socialize.

A Teaching Tolerance project of the Southern Poverty Law Center advocates "Mix-It-Up at Lunch" days, where students sit wherever they want in the cafeteria, with people they usually avoid or ignore. Its purpose is noble and a critical element of responsive, responsible schools. "Mix It Up is a nationwide campaign that supports students who want to identify, question, and cross social boundaries that separate them from each other and help build inclusive, welcoming learning environments" ("Anyone Can Mix It Up!" 2008, p. 32). This is a powerful approach, especially for middle-childhood-age students, because tolerance begins with getting to know the other person as a person—not as a label or a category. The attention you give daily to such things as seating arrangements, cooperative groups, and partner work, subtly and steadily breaks down the barriers children use to separate themselves from each other.

At what age do you have to worry about bullying in your classroom? Relational bullying starts as early as pre-kindergarten, as children tell others they can't play and announce that they aren't someone's friend anymore. These rejections are hurtful and for some classrooms the bully, observer, and victim roles becomes entrenched.

Vivian Gussin Paley takes the problem of rejection and bullying to heart, so much so that she wrote a book about her efforts. She witnessed this unjust structure of haves and have-nots develop in the kindergarten classes she taught and watched it become more and more entrenched as the children moved through school. As expressed in her book *You Can't Say You Can't Play*, Ms. Paley's realization is a simple and disturbing one: "Certain children will have the right to limit the social experiences of their classmates. . . . Long after hitting and name-calling have been outlawed by the teachers, a more damaging phenomenon is allowed to take root, spreading like a weed from grade to grade" (1992, p. 3). She did something about it by making a new classroom rule: You can't say you can't play. Her book chronicles her experiences trying to change the social culture of her school.

Intentionally selecting the makeup of groups, or randomly pulling Popsicle sticks from a jar, grouping by colors, and so on, done regularly soon stirs things up so much it becomes part of the norm in your classroom for students to work with every one of their classmates. With your constant, caring oversight, you can help these groupings succeed and hence foster acceptance and even new friendships. You also clearly live the belief that we are all of equal worth.

The caution against letting students choose their own partners or groups is self-evident. Through your empathetic eye, you can see what a negative practice this is for children. This one act can thwart your goal of establishing a climate of acceptance and emotional safety. By arranging random or teacher-determined groupings you remove the social anxiety and stigma of being left out or last chosen. It lets students safely get down to the tasks at hand: learning the academic curriculum and practicing getting along with each other. You must, though, have a serious discussion with your class about this or a "you can't say you can't play" approach beforehand. You are not dictating with whom a child should be friends; you are saying that in this classroom (or school), we all respect and work with each other. There is no place for rejection.

Thinking Activity: Empathy in Everyday Classroom Life

Ask your students to imagine a situation where groups are being chosen for a social studies project. The teacher has chosen group leaders and they are to select the member of their groups. Ask your students to stand in the shoes of the child who is often excluded, and who waits to be chosen. Ask them these questions: What is he feeling? What is going through his mind? Then change the perspective by asking them to consider how the team leaders are feeling.

Explain to them that what they were expressing is a feeling called *empathy*— the ability to put yourself in someone else's place and see and feel as they would. Talk about what it feels like to have others react negatively—verbally, with facial expressions, body language, or attitude—when the partners or groups are announced or gathered to work. Ask them to describe the respectful way to react when announcements are made for partners or groups. Have a conversation about how they should treat their partner and teammates, no matter who they are.

Some children already have a sensitive, empathetic nature and take to this way of thinking easily. For others, who are less inclined to be introspective or who have never been asked to think this way before, this may be a brand new, eye-opening way of looking at things. Some might be skeptical of accepting and including all the students as equals. In this case, teach and diligently re-

---

REFLECTION: FIFTH GRADE

My cooperating teacher and I are getting ready for me to take over. Today I arranged the students' seating, and I thought it was going to be easy. The more I worked at it I realized I wanted students to be away from others who would cause problems, and I considered how to make a student feel comfortable. An example would be not to have a boy at an all-girl cluster of tables. It will be interesting to watch and see if the seating arrangement will be a good one or not, especially when some students do not normally talk with each other in the classroom.

---

inforce what a kind response looks and sounds like, until it becomes second nature for your students to show respect and concern for each other—every single member of *each other.*

CHILDREN ARE STILL LEARNING

In the flurry of teaching and all the extraneous responsibilities that come with it, we may forget this simple premise: Children are still learning. Holding regular meetings is a good way to slow down the frenzy and give students a chance to practice those important social skills and learn new attitudes. They also remind us to be patient teachers.

Solving problems, expressing appreciation, learning communication skills, celebrating successes, and planning activities can all be accomplished through a simple, defined process called a *class meeting.* Jane Nelsen advanced the concept of regular, structured class meetings as a means of teaching critical pro-social skills in her book *Positive Discipline.*

As defined by Nelson, every class meeting begins with an opportunity for members to express appreciation for kindnesses. This enables students to recognize the help and support they give each other. The class meeting continues with agenda items suggested by students and the teacher, usually problems or concerns that need resolution. The "owner" of the problem leads the discussion and solicits ideas from classmates. At the end of the discussion, the owner shares which ideas she will try. At the next meeting the students are asked to share what they tried and how things are going. Nelsen describes this process in detail in chapter 7 of *Positive Discipline.*

As the students explore real-life problems in this thoughtful way, they practice expressing concerns calmly, listening respectfully and patiently to the ideas of others, and exploring constructive ways to resolve problems. Students experience the transformational power of a genuine team effort and learn how it feels to be part of a supportive community. From my own

---

REFLECTION: FIFTH GRADE

I had a surprise yesterday. A new student was to arrive today. She came this morning and things went well. We had a class meeting to introduce ourselves and tell about our favorite things. The students are now asking to have our class meeting before I can even call them to the rug.

---

experience, class meetings quickly become a treasured part of classroom life, so much so that students may choose to pass up a scheduled recess to fit in a meeting! The class meeting process teaches us to tolerate ambiguity. We learn there isn't one right answer to every problem. There are many perspectives on the same concerns and we benefit by listening to new ideas and trying them out. One of the revelations of class meetings was discovering that some children who are usually quiet or not the most successful at schoolwork excel in practical, caring problem solving. In this forum they find their voice and gain a new level of appreciation and respect from their teachers and peers.

Class meetings feel good and are helpful in so many ways. When we validate and attend to real-life issues that are important to children, they become engaged. Engaged children pay attention, internalize, and grow from the experience. This attention and practice, over many years of schooling, teaches them critical skills and attitudes that serve them well in life. As play is the "work" of children, class meetings are practice for a responsible adulthood. My experience using class meetings in second grade and with adults in graduate classes and seminars taught me how powerful you feel as part of a tight, caring community. The deep level of connection you reach with each other is awe-inspiring.

Class meetings give students a chance to practice pro-social skills:

- Listening respectfully when others speak
- Brainstorming ideas
- Giving and receiving compliments
- Dealing honestly with problems
- Problem solving
- Accepting different speaking styles and ways of thinking
- Considering the point of view of others
- Reflecting the mood of others
- Feeling and showing empathy
- Giving positive feedback
- Taking turns
- Including each person in the process

- Respecting the rights of individuals and the group
- Compromising to reach an agreement
- Making and keeping agreements

Class meetings also give students a chance to practice verbal skills:

- Clearly articulating a need or concern
- Expressing feelings
- Asking questions to clarify
- Offering solutions
- Asking for help
- Expressing appreciation to others
- Staying on topic
- Choosing wording that is respectful and helpful

REFLECTION: FOURTH GRADE

Today was my second in the fourth-grade class. We had recess inside our classroom. This gave me a great chance to see how my students interact socially. I was shocked at how many little "cliques" have formed. There were two groups, one of boys and one of girls, that would not let others join in their group. I tried to interject but when I stepped in the other kid no longer wanted to play with the others. My teacher told me that this is a serious problem, especially with the girls, that they have every year. This is something that I know I must monitor every day.

How observant and wise this student teacher was. Part of my response to her concerns was to suggest that if this is a serious problem every year, they should have a proactive prevention plan to make sure it doesn't continue, and that class meetings would help.

GENERIC TEACHING STRATEGIES GO A LONG WAY

To go along with class meetings, here are some ideas for how to teach in a culturally responsive way. Regularly use generic teaching strategies and attitudes that . . .

- Embed respect for diversity into the academic curriculum.
- Teach critical pro-social life and thinking skills.
- Prepare students for a diverse world!

As teachers . . .

- Seize every opportunity to stress understanding and appreciation of differences.
- Convey the message that *every* student can participate in and enjoy any academic or extracurricular pursuit she chooses, regardless of gender, background, socioeconomic status, race, or ethnicity.
- Choose instructional materials and experiences that are culturally diverse, gender-stereotype free; that broaden students' perspectives of the world; and that incorporate underrepresented groups.
- Model anti-bias attitudes and behaviors, and teach and expect respect for each other.
- Present collaborative, community-building, noncompetitive games and challenges.
- Organize classroom, school, and community service projects.
- Remember that children do not respond well to teasing—well-intentioned or not—because teasing is a power play and usually has a core of truth. It is hurtful (to adults as well).
- Use instructional strategies that encourage student interaction such as cooperative learning groups, partnering, buddy systems, peer teaching, think-pair-share, and mixed-age groupings.
- Give students a chance to show what they know and can do in a variety of ways, and assess student learning using these approaches.
- Teach perspective by taking the other point of view on issues, events, problems.
- Regularly bring regional and world cultures into the classroom through the arts, current events and literature, social studies, science, and math.

Have students . . .

- Compare/contrast historical perspectives by *groups* of people (Native Americans/settlers, males/females, workers/bosses, etc.).
- Take on the persona of a character from literature or history; role play or write a journal entry to reflect how that character would view a certain situation or event.
- Read and compare a variety of primary historical documents from different individuals, groups, and times (e.g., journals, letters, diaries, political cartoons, newspaper articles, and editorials)
- Write position papers and justify positions.
- Read biographies and autobiographies of people of both genders and diverse cultural backgrounds, and look for common themes such as courage, dignity, adversity, family, integrity.

- Conduct personal interviews of a cross section of people about an issue or topic.
- Research the time period when a book was written and predict how society might have influenced the author.
- Explore and celebrate students' family heritages and traditions.

REFLECTION: SECOND GRADE

I'll tell you about something that happened today during the lesson, since I think you'll appreciate this story more than a math one. In my classroom, when students raise their hand to get a drink, go to the bathroom, or get a tissue, they have to do it with a sign language letter (*d* for *drink*, and so on). Well, naturally, it's taken me a while to get used to this, since I didn't know any sign language a month ago (I know three letters now).

Anyway, a student had his hand up, and I wasn't calling on him, not realizing his hand was up with the sign letter *T* for *tissue*. So, another kid raises his hand to answer a question (or so I thought). Instead, he asked to get a tissue. I said yes, and I saw him go get one and then hand it to the other boy who had his hand up. It made me think adults could really learn a lot from kids. Plus, everyone made out in the end—the boy got his tissue, and I gave the helper, who I was so touched by, an activity pad. Thought you'd enjoy that story.

I did enjoy it. It is one of those memorable teaching anecdotes that shows us how amazingly perceptive and helpful students are.

RESPECT IS SOMETHING YOU CAN SEE

This awareness of the needs and perspectives of others plays a part in all relationships within a school community. Here are some universal themes and beliefs about what respect means, as seen from different perspectives, brainstormed by my elementary school faculty.

Toward colleagues:

- Asking, not assuming
- Going to the source for information
- Being willing to listen
- Giving time, help, and support
- Sharing ideas
- Having a sense of humor
- Being aware of individual needs

- Showing empathy, care, and concern
- Maintaining a climate free of intimidation
- Using cooperative problem-solving
- Looking at the problem, not at the person

Toward students:

- Actively listening
- Providing them the freedom to make choices
- Giving them responsibility
- Accepting individual differences and circumstances
- Modeling politeness
- Validating students' feelings and what they are telling us
- Building on strengths
- Recognizing accomplishments
- Cooperating and being flexible
- Using authority with compassion
- Developing rules together

Toward ourselves:

- Accepting ourselves for who we are
- Acknowledging our strengths and where we can improve
- Emphasizing the positive
- Doing nice things for ourselves
- Refusing to accept disrespect
- Standing up for ourselves
- Taking time for personal reflection
- Respecting others
- Doing our best
- Being honest with ourselves and others
- Showing empathy
- Having high standards
- Taking pride in what we do
- Listening to what our heart says
- Remembering that other points of view exist

Toward parents:

- Building a trusting relationship with parents
- Working to alleviate negative past experiences
- Sharing positive comments by phone, notes, and in person

- Communicating about concerns and successes regularly
- Considering parents' opinions and input
- Understanding family pressures and that the nature of families has changed
- Reporting a child's progress in an appropriate and meaningful way
- Welcoming and including parents as active participants in their child's education
- Responding to communications from students' families
- Talking about parents respectfully, and in private
- Asking parents what they think and for their help

Toward administrators:

- Attending meetings
- Valuing others and their input
- Giving all ideas sincere consideration
- Following the chain of command
- Following through on your word
- Acting on your commitments
- Trusting (which inspires risk taking)
- Understanding the administrator's complex role
- Considering everyone's needs
- Taking responsibility for your actions

Toward the community:

- Listening to their concerns
- Keeping them informed
- Making them part of our plans
- Asking them for help and input
- Keeping ourselves informed of important concerns that they have
- Participating in community activities
- Having students involved in their own neighborhood communities
- Encouraging use of the school facilities
- Inviting them into the school to volunteer and for performances
- Recognizing and using the assets of the community

We now see how character education, violence prevention, and multicultural education are not done justice if handled as discrete programs. They are meant to work together as an expression of your internal belief system that shows in everything you do, say, and teach. Essential Understanding 8 presents another way successful teachers bring this high level of relevance and authenticity to their work in the classroom.

Essential Understanding 8

Teaching Is Like Acting: Know Your Material Well, Show Enthusiasm, and Have Fun!

REFLECTION: SECOND GRADE

One thing I've noticed is that my energy level is great. Even if I am dead tired, I can still get into a lesson and (hopefully) make it interesting because the students can see that I am actually interested in what I am doing. I think they saw it today with something as simple as Morning Meeting.

IS THERE A HAM IN YOU?

Consider the college classes you enjoyed attending and the ones that you would do anything to avoid. In one, time flew, and in the other, it was all you could do to stay awake. Absent any extenuating circumstances such as an extreme of time of day, the variable is the teacher and what he does to make the subject matter enjoyable and relevant.

You teach best what you know and are excited about, and there is no substitute for being well prepared *and* flexible. You never know when something will come up and you will have to improvise. The best-designed lesson presented in a lackluster way with little confidence will most likely fall flat.

To make sure this isn't how you teach, think of yourself as an actor and the classroom as your stage. The audience expects your best performance each day. Like a stage actor, your voice is your best teaching tool—use it to your advantage. Monitor the volume, rate, and pitch of your voice. A voice that is too soft or too loud becomes an impediment to learning, something to tune out. Body language plays an important role, too. Convey the message that you are happy to be teaching your students and are confident that they will cooperate with you. Be creative and animated—use props, songs, and drama to energize your students!

Recall how in Essential Understanding 3 we said that if we expect the best from our students they usually rise to the occasion. Do not give the impression that you are afraid of them, that you are at a loss for what to do, or that you have had it with their behavior and are giving up. Do not sit at your desk and do not act like the material is boring. I've heard teachers say to their students, "I know this is boring but we have to go through it."

Early on in your teaching experience ask a supervisor or mentor if there is anything you can do to improve your teaching voice, your body language, and your oral teaching style. Find out if any students in the class have auditory processing or hearing problems and brainstorm ways to assist them. Do this for visual challenges and other learning needs as well.

WHAT ARE *YOU* DOING?

It is absolutely crucial that you resist the urge to *blame* the students, their parents, society, television, pop music, the school administration, the teachers in the grade below you, the federal government, and so on if your lessons are not going well and the students aren't paying attention. Acknowledge these influences, and then look closer to home—at yourself, your specific students, and the classroom setting where you have power to make a change. Blaming is unproductive and only increases your frustration and sense of helplessness. It also leads to cynicism and burnout.

If the students are not attentive or lose focus as the lesson progresses, avoid being quick to point a blaming finger. It is time to regroup and ask yourself why they aren't attentive or "getting it." Evaluate your own behavior and instructional choices and see what you can do to improve your instruction. This is the empowered way to approach the challenges of teaching. It maintains your sense of efficacy.

Some factors to consider:

- Is the learning personally relevant to your students?
- Are you lecturing, expecting them to just sit and listen?
- How is the tone of your voice? Is it lackluster and monotone or too loud and piercing?
- Is the material too difficult or too easy for some or most of the students?
- Do they have the necessary prior knowledge to succeed at the task?

- Is the lesson too long for their developmental level?
- Have you differentiated the materials to meet special needs?
- Are you unsure of the material you are teaching?
- Are you not feeling as well as usual or are you in a bad mood? (It happens!)
- Did you underestimate how long the lesson would take and find yourself rushing to beat the clock?
- Did they just come back from physical education class, recess, or an exciting assembly?
- Did they just finish taking a stressful standardized test?

A good teacher reflects and analyzes why things go well and not so well and avoids placing blame. That includes not blaming yourself. It is counterproductive and misdirects your mental energies. It also provides an excuse to not take responsibility for doing better next time. Holding yourself and others responsible is not the same as blaming. With this approach you acknowledge that an issue exists and you deal with it. To the contrary, a blaming lens puts the onus on others and requires no personal effort toward improvement. When you blame yourself, you are taking on a discouraged view. Remember how we said previously that students need to be able to take risks and rally from setbacks? So do teachers.

REFLECTION: FIFTH GRADE

As I'm nearing my final weeks here I am dreading leaving. I have never been in a classroom before where the kids are so polite and helpful of one another. I am going to be heartbroken when I leave. I know I will be making plenty of visits back to this class.

We had a decent science lesson today that the kids got into. I talked about frogs and how they eat and swallow and I used a lot of facial expressions and movements and used words like "gross" and "nasty" in reference to frogs eating bugs alive without chewing it and the kids loved it! They got right into it and they started asking questions and got into the sound effects and motions too! I left the lesson telling them that on Monday we would be seeing some digestion and they wanted to see it now. They wanted to know what it was but all I said was that it would involve stealing my dad's lunch and now they're psyched!

I'm finally getting the hang of better hooks and closings. I've been using lots of discussions to get things started or finished and it works!

REFLECTION: SIXTH GRADE

Since lately I feel that I have been hammering my students with facts about science and have not performed a demonstration in a couple days, I wanted to change my lesson up and do something fun. Since our last lesson focused on color, I thought it would be fun to have the students make their own sun catchers.

To do this I went out and bought different color cellophane and solid clear backgrounds. The students were instructed to take the pieces of cellophane and make a design on the solid clear background. The design would then be covered with clear cellophane to protect their design. I am putting the sun catchers on the window so that their work can be displayed to the class and to show the students that I am proud of the effort they put into their sun catchers.

But, since I wanted to make sure that the students were still learning something during this fun lesson, I had each one write the primary colors that they used. Since the cellophane was the primary colors, the answer to that question was simple. I also had the students describe what colors they made with the primary colors. I did that because I wanted the students to see that many colors can be made when mixing just a couple colors together.

Also, I wanted to incorporate math into this lesson so I had the students write down the fractional components of each color they used. I felt like this was a good idea and an easy way to connect other subjects into one lesson. Tomorrow when I begin teaching my science lesson, I am going to review what the students learned from making their sun catchers before moving on to the next topic.

That's it! Make your teaching compelling to watch. Actively engage your students in meaningful learning experiences. Your students deserve your best, and to do your best you have to be well prepared and enthusiastic. After you have done all the preparation for a great lesson, set your objectives, researched your content, designed the activities, and created and collected the materials, you should feel well prepared to teach the lesson and also excited to teach it. From my personal experience and in watching hundreds of classroom lessons, I can say without hesitation that, in addition to the concepts, vocabulary, and facts, it is critical that teachers know the big-picture ideas of the content and how the lesson advances students toward their goals and objectives.

Knowing your content, having your materials ready, and making the learning relevant and engaging have a big payoff: fewer discipline problems and better student learning. Not being prepared is the slippery slope to teacher meltdown.

Instructional materials should be prepared well ahead of time, organized and easy to find, so the teacher can be ready to greet the students when they arrive at the door. Two minutes before class starts is no time to make last-minute copies or scramble to find enough rulers for the math lesson.

REFLECTION: FIFTH GRADE

Today felt like a rough day. It takes so long for this class and the other class to get settled and ready to learn. I feel like I did give them quite a bit of leeway today. Math is very difficult because I do not feel comfortable with it yet. My teacher and I had decided to wait to introduce fractions until later in the week. Then this morning after talking with her more she decided that maybe we should do it today. So at the last minute I had to come up with a way to get them interested in fractions. She would usually just wing it. I cannot do that. So I went down to the library and found a book on fractions to read to them. It was okay. They have done fractions before many times so this is so redundant. Tomorrow I will do something with fractions that is part of the Investigations curriculum. I do not feel very confident about it. We will see how it goes.

What happened here? Learning took a backseat this morning, and the honest answer is that the teacher was responsible. He was having a bad day. He is the adult, the professional, the role model, and he wasn't prepared to teach—yet he expects his students to come to class prepared with all the materials they need, homework done, and a good attitude. His frustration with the situation and obvious distraction led to students fooling around and his display of misplaced anger. The relationship between him and his students was damaged, his authority has been undermined, and valuable time has been lost. Now think about ways the teacher could have avoided the situation or handled it better. If this kind of thing ever happens to you, handle it calmly and reasonably, and give students something meaningful to do. Preserve your relationship by offering the class a sincere apology for wasting their time. You will earn respect in their eyes.

Thinking Activity: The Set-Up

Read the following scenario and reflect on *what* happened, *why* it happened, and *who* was responsible for what happened.

Scenario: You get off to a slow start one morning and arrive at the classroom later than usual only to discover you can't find your lesson plan and materials for the first class of the day. You start looking in your school bag and on your desk. The students watch you and wait quietly for a minute. Soon they start to talk among themselves. A few are getting loud and out of their seats. Some empathetic students come over and volunteer to help you find what you are looking for. You thank them and send them back to their seats as you continue trying to find your missing materials.

You are feeling annoyed and are losing patience for the students' increasingly unsettled behavior. You give a distracted and loud "Quiet down!" but they continue on unsupervised and get noisier while you again search through the piles of paper on the counter. You are now agitated and yell at them, "Sit down and stop talking!" You write a child's name on the board, then another's. Your frustration is clearly mounting and the students notice. Not a moment too soon, you find the missing materials under some books you borrowed from the library. Now it is time for you and the students to switch gears and start the lesson—but you are thrown, you've lost ten minutes of teaching time, and the students are unfocused and defensive.

YOU CAN BE CONTAGIOUS!

REFLECTION: FIFTH GRADE

Today I actually made social studies fun. I demonstrated to the class how the British took over New Amsterdam without firing a shot. I had two girls, each armed with one small paper ball, be New Amsterdam. I had the rest of the class surround them, each with three or four large paper balls. I told them the paper balls were cannons and asked the girls who were New Amsterdam what they would do. One girl said fight, which is what the governor wanted to do, and the other said surrender, what the colonists wanted to do. I felt this was a perfect demonstration of this event in history and I hope they remember it for a long time.

We also did an activity where I had them write one or two sentences about me. Then I asked who wrote I was the greatest teacher ever. I told the rest of the class they lost recess for the rest of the year. I explained that I was the king of this class and no one will write bad things about me. I felt this was a perfect lead into our discussion of freedom of the press.

A seamless meshing of classroom instruction and classroom management is a matter of cause and effect. It is a cycle with each impacting the other. Starting off with interesting lessons and spirited teaching leads to better behavior and allows you to do more interesting, spirited teaching. You are a beginning teacher, which means you will be required to teach subjects and skills that you have never taught before and that may not be your favorites. It is time to make them your favorites or at least learn to like them! If you are bored, uninspired, and unsure of what you are teaching you can count on your students to be the same—and to act out in a variety of ways.

To get started on mastering the curriculum, children's trade books and grade-level materials are a valuable simple introduction to the topic. This level of resources gives a basic foundation of concepts and vocabulary. Next, read more sophisticated materials intended for older students and adults, speak with colleagues, and search the Internet for lesson ideas and good websites to use for instruction. Using a lesson plan on the topic that you come across is fine; it isn't plagiarism. Lessons posted on teacher websites and included in printed materials are meant to be used, and it shows you are smart enough to recognize a good lesson when you see one. Teachers are historically generous with materials and ideas, and great resources can be found in the classroom next door. Just ask. To boost your enthusiasm for the topic, take the lesson and materials and put your own spin on them. Make them dynamic to fit your personality and teaching style. These fine-tunings can carry the lesson and convey your enjoyment of the topic.

It is common for student and beginning teachers to say they never liked science (or math, etc.) and that they wished they didn't have to teach it—only to have them discover how fascinating and doable it is once they have processed it in a way that makes sense to them. One of the perks of teaching is that you get to master an array of knowledge and skills in areas you might have once shunned or felt inept at. It is testament to the old adage that the best way to learn something is to teach it. When you operate on the *metacognitive* level—thinking about what you are learning—and teach the content with enthusiasm and confidence, your students develop a positive attitude toward the subject matter. Your genuine enthusiasm and knowledge is infectious, and the students actively engage and learn in a way that sticks.

REFLECTION: KINDERGARTEN

Today was the last day of my space unit and as the culminating activity we went on a moon walk. The children had been working on their space crowns in art class for the last two weeks, and we made space suits out of white garbage bags so we looked like real astronauts! Then I rubber-banded sponges to the bottom of everyone's feet and we walked around the outside of the school talking about how the sponges felt and how the real moon would feel. The children were so excited to go on the moon walk and wear their space suits.

We also talked about gravity all week and today we talked about how astronauts have to eat out of bags. So we made pudding in zip lock bags and cut the corners and ate pudding like real astronauts! I think I enjoyed watching the children as much as they enjoyed doing it. They really learned a lot about space in the past two weeks, and a moon walk was a great way to end the unit. I am really sad that my solo week and unit is done; I have learned so much and enjoyed watching the children learn so much through hands-on experiences.

The wonder of a thematic, cohesive instructional unit taught over time is the level of involvement reached by both the children and the teacher. Immersion is *the* way to teach! By becoming an expert on the content and overarching concepts, you can use this high level of understanding of the content to develop a series of effective, engaging, developmentally appropriate lessons. As you organize and teach your sequence of lessons, ask yourself a few questions:

- Who is doing most of the work in the lessons? Who is thinking and talking? The answer should be the students. True, you do work hard, with much of your effort going to designing quality learning experiences and facilitating your students' construction of knowledge and understanding.
- Are the lessons relevant to the students personally? Learning that sticks is all about making connections—the Velcro approach we will discuss in the next Essential Understanding. Make sure you have planned ways for the students to get involved in the activities and connect to the ideas and information. This is a constructivist approach and the basis of motivation.
- Are the methods of instruction and materials developmentally appropriate for the range of student abilities and special needs? You have to anticipate the behavior and cognitive level of children at various stages of development in general and for your class in particular. Plan wisely by identifying these needs and differentiating your materials and expectations accordingly.
- How did the lessons go? How effective were they in teaching the concepts, knowledge, and skills you intended? When a lesson is over, reflect on what went well and what did not. As warranted, revise the content, the materials, and your instructional methods . . . and then try again. This is the process of metacognition as applied to lesson design and implementation.

The process of self-evaluating as you create and teach your lessons keeps you fresh, keeps your students interested and achieving, and makes your classroom a place where students want to be. Not every teacher shows a natural inclination or the self-confidence to be theatrical. It may be hidden inside you

---

REFLECTION: PRE-K

I still feel like I could show a little more excitement when I am teaching. My voice sounds a bit boring on the tape. I had good projection of my voice when talking one-on-one with students and when addressing other students who were playing within the classroom.

REFLECTION: FIFTH GRADE

I had told the students yesterday that if all of them completed their homework for today we could watch the video that I did for my evaluation. They were thrilled and with a few exceptions all of them completed their homework. They were excited all day about watching the video. I thought what better way to teach than have them see how they learn and interact with each other. They watched and had a great time. They are going to write up a critique of how they worked with their kindergarten writing-buddies.

waiting to be unleashed. You can develop this side of you if you recognize that acting is what successful teachers do. Start by experimenting with voices as your read stories to the class, share personal anecdotes, and do something unexpected or silly. Ham it up using facial expressions, humor, and lots of movement. It is easier to do this in front of children than adults. Children are very accepting of your genuine and not-so-polished attempts. Videotape yourself teaching and see how you look and sound to your students. This is one of the most effective ways to see your strengths and honestly face your areas of weakness. The same goes for your students.

Part of the magic of teaching is a phenomenon that happens when your students enter your classroom. Good teachers who are self-aware and committed

REFLECTION: SECOND GRADE

Another special activity I had planned for the children today was to teach them about communication. We wrote the definition in their social studies notebooks and then I asked them to put them away so that they would have nothing on their desks. As I waited for them to quiet down, I walked around the room with my finger up to my mouth showing them that I wanted them to be quiet. Some caught on quickly, but I snuck up behind others and when they turned around they saw what I was doing. Some of the students giggled as I snuck up on those who were still chatting, but it only took about 3 minutes to quiet the whole class down.

Even when I took my finger off my mouth, the children who had a question to ask whispered it to me. This was a simple brainstorm that I had as a way to get them to quiet down quickly without raising my voice. When I had all of their attention I spoke in almost a whisper and asked them to join me in a circle on the floor in back. They thought this was really cool.

to a positive classroom climate click into another gear—their onstage teacher mode—and with the right attitude that mode can be upbeat and energizing. As you face a sea of expectant faces, a captive audience that you are responsible for, your instincts kick in and the children become your priority. No matter what happened at home that morning, how bad the traffic was, or your worries about a sick relative, you know that you must put it all behind you and concentrate on making your students' day a productive and pleasant one. The very act of being positive and smiling improves your attitude. Rising to the occasion helps ensure that you and your students get a high-quality classroom experience every day.

Teachers come into the profession wanting to be free to enjoy themselves and the children, and to look forward to coming to school. They want to stay in teaching and have a satisfying career.

To make this a reality, you need to be taken seriously as a teacher—one who is respected and listened to—and still able to have fun teaching. Here is a simple tip you can implement from day one that helps your lessons go smoothly, with fewer interruptions, and lets you and the students relax in the classroom. When directing or redirecting students, make statements rather than ask questions. And never ask a question you don't want an answer to, or threaten something you cannot and really do not want to do! Some examples:

- "Can you sit in your seats now?" invites the student looking for an easy laugh from his classmates to shout, "No!"
- "Why do you keep bothering your partner?" opens up the opportunity for the student with behavior issues to argue with you over *who* is actually bothering *whom.*
- "If you continue to talk I'm never going to read aloud to you again" is a hollow threat you cannot keep and the children know it. It weakens your authority and isn't an effective way to help them improve their behavior.

It is easier to avoid these common new teacher mistakes if you keep your wits about you when you are frustrated and recognize and use your personal and positional power. Fight the fear that you are losing control of the room by staying in control of yourself. Monitor your breathing, voice, body language, choice of words, and use of statements instead of questions. Some suggestions are:

- "I need everyone's attention up here on me. Thank you" replaces the unassertive "Can you put your crayons away and look up here?"
- A quiet, in private, "You both know the rules for working in groups. Please start taking turns doing the experiment" replaces the ineffective, frustrated "Can you two stop grabbing the cubes from each other?"

- "Before we start using the microscopes, let's review our rules for using science equipment" replaces the unreasonable and unenforceable "If you can't handle the materials correctly we'll just read from the textbook from now on."

The vast majority of children do have a desire to please adults and they respond well to acknowledgments and appreciation for specific things. This is not the same as offering generic praise like the overused "Good job," which tells the child nothing about the specific behavior you wish to reinforce. It is akin to patting a dog on the head and saying, "Good boy!"

Thank your students and reinforce their good choices with encouraging words and written notes. Be specific. "Thank you for volunteering to put the rulers back in the closet after math" replaces "You're great!" Contrary to common practice, you do not need candy, stickers, stars, marbles in a jar, or prizes from a treasure chest to motivate children; a smile, handshake, compliment, acknowledgment, and small celebrations of your classroom community as a whole are asset builders that have a profound effect on your students' attitude toward themselves and school, and on the classroom climate you are able to establish. A twenty-minute Friday "game time" with simple snacks gives the message that we are a cohesive community, like a family, and that we like each other's company and can have fun together—all of us, not just a select few who reached some artificial criteria we have set.

Again thinking back to Glasser's five basic needs, participating as a full member of the group can have a positive effect on a student's sense of self-worth, and her fortitude to try to do better. It meets her needs to belong, have fun, exercise freedom, and feel powerful. Throw in some popcorn and you have also met the need for survival!

Remember that you are on stage and that you teach best what you know and are excited about, especially when you teach it in a way that meets every student's basic needs. Be well prepared and teach with energy and enthusiasm in a way students learn best. And, as we will see in Essential Understanding 9, using your students' natural inclinations adds to your effectiveness.

It Is Counterproductive to Fight Human Nature: Put It To Work for You Instead

Thinking Activity: Human Nature in Your Own Life

Think about your own life and jot down some ideas for each of these questions.

- What do you like to do in your free time?
- What kind of classes and workshops do you appreciate most?
- How did you learn how to do the hobbies you enjoy?
- What does it look like when you get together with a group of friends?

Now, take a look at your responses and identify the aspects they have in common. Keep these in mind as you read these reflections about this essential understanding.

REFLECTION: THIRD GRADE

I taught a math lesson about four as a factor today. The lesson did not go as well as I had hoped. We used counters as manipulatives and the kids seemed to be more focused on the counters than the concepts. I realize now that I need to establish ground rules for using counters. They are tools not toys. Even maybe letting them play with the counters for a few minutes to get it out of their system would have been fine. I also should be more forceful with the kids when I am teaching. I then need to hold them accountable. When I finished, I felt like the strategies were too difficult and I should simplify the review. But now, I feel that they perhaps were not focused enough because I did not establish my authority. This lesson was a tremendous learning experience.

This is metacognition at its finest! You can feel the internal conversation the student teacher is engaged in as she thinks back on the lesson. Here is how I responded to this thoughtful reflection: "*Yes*! That's exactly what they need. It's a wise person who sees when it is better to legitimize unwanted behavior than to fight it! It is natural for them to want to play with manipulatives. They also need to be able to get down to serious work when you tell them to."

I have watched new teachers and veterans try fruitlessly to keep students from talking and moving around while they are learning. They spend a good deal of their precious and limited instructional time shushing students and "waiting for them to be quiet." Shushing is overused and can take on an angry and impatient tone. It usually means something is going on that warrants your closer attention. Standing in front of the students with your arms crossed and a scowl on your face, telling them you will just wait for them to stop talking, is actually a passive approach that can backfire on you. It becomes a stare-down, a test of wills. Do you really want the students to determine when and for how long you can teach them? Are you really willing to wait for however long it takes for them to settle down, without intervening? What does this practice do to the climate in the classroom and to the students' sense of respect and security?

A more effective approach might be to tell the class they have one minute to finish talking to their neighbor, after which the lesson starts. (A timer comes in handy.) This approach builds cooperation and trust as they come to view you as a reasonable teacher who works *with* them rather than against them. This small accommodation of their basic need to talk with their peers is not a threat to your authority. It is an affirmation of your professionalism and skills.

REFLECTION: FIRST GRADE

The kids were off the wall today. They couldn't sit still or stop talking. I think it was because the first part of the day we did straight work for about an hour and this wasn't fun for them. I tried to break up the work by playing Simon Says, and then by doing some stretches. This helped for about 10 minutes. I feel like these kids sat for a long time. I would have been acting like that, too. That's why I really like learning stations because they are doing the academics but then they rotate to new centers so it isn't all the same thing for an hour. I think doing centers with little kids really helps out.

REFLECTION: FIRST GRADE

Today's math lesson went well. I had the students fill in a new shape with blocks and then we discussed how to total the amount of shapes used. The students are learning the shape names and using them a lot during the lesson when speaking to me and to other students. I love to hear the conversation that goes on during these lessons. The students are always on task discussing their use of blocks versus their neighbors'.

A simple lesson such as this one is a perfect example of how to take a proactive approach whenever possible to avoid fighting human nature. By using what we know children enjoy and need as the legitimate and effective teaching methods they are, we are working with their natural inclinations. Children like to talk, play with new things, and work together—so go ahead and design your lessons with ample opportunity to do this. Let them explore new manipulatives, maps, books, and so on before first trying to use them for instruction, and let them talk with each other as they learn. Think of all the verbal reprimands and shushing this avoids. Children dislike being embarrassed in front of others, being singled out, and not being listened to. They are more motivated to cooperate with you if you treat them fairly. Set them up for success. Work with them and their natural instincts. As we emphasized before, if you didn't like the teacher telling everyone to work in silence when you were a child, or even a college student, then don't do it to your students.

There are no pat answers to all the dilemmas, large and small, that teachers face every day. Making a good decision requires an analysis of the situation and a keen understanding of children's needs. Hands-on activities are motivating and bring out a natural desire to talk, at which point exuberance sometimes trumps following the rules! At times it is fine to have students speak without raising their hands, especially when you are doing something that is meant to excite them. Let them be spontaneous. At other times it is important for students to listen quietly. In all situations, avoid over- or under-controlling.

Another chance to work with, not against, human nature is to recognize that intense physical and social activity is often followed by hunger, thirst, and fatigue that can only be satisfied by nourishment and rest. One early childhood education student teacher had a problem settling her children down for math after recess (as we noted before, a common challenge). They came in the room hot and thirsty with flushed, sweaty faces; their hearts were beating wildly. After playing hard, they needed a period of transition before she tried an organized learning activity.

We discussed what was happening and thought she should try a new approach: Have the lights off and soft music playing when they come in, and let them get a drink and wash up before they sit down on the rug. She tried this child-friendly approach and happily discovered that after a drink, some cool water on their faces, and a gentle song or a short story, they were relaxed and ready for math. This became her after-recess routine, and it turned a stressful time for her and the children into one to look forward to. She was done fighting human nature. It took a willingness to look at the situation from the students' point of view and to analyze the role the teacher played. She didn't give in. Her openness showed her desire to help the children do better, an understanding of human needs, and a willingness to be flexible and try something different. Everyone benefited.

This story is an example of using brain-friendly, developmentally appropriate, logical approaches to solving problems. Now take out your responses to the questions posed at the beginning of the chapter. What *do* you do in your free time? What kind of learning activities and hobbies do you like? How do you learn best? What commonalities did you discover? Keep these in mind as you read the following list of brain-friendly experiences. See how your list compares with this one.

THE BRAIN LOVES . . .

When working to create a positive school climate and successful learning experiences, remember that the brain loves . . .

- Talking
- Feeling safe
- Social interaction
- Movement
- Real-world experiences
- Visuals/color
- Challenge and hard work
- Making connections
- Rhyme
- Music and rhythm
- Stories and storytelling
- Finding meaning
- Novelty

What a fun list! Picture learning experiences with these components and imagine how engaged you'd be. Now think how motivating it would be for children to learn by these methods.

Providing ample time to explore ideas and materials; dialogue that allows for personal connections; activities that get children talking to each other, moving around, singing and tapping their feet, chanting and clapping—all help to make the experience meaningful and memorable. And not by coincidence these brain-friendly practices satisfy the realms of the 4MAT Learning Cycle (which we will soon discuss), the five basic needs, various learning styles and temperaments, gender-based learning differences, and everything we know about positive discipline and respect for diversity!

Each lesson does not require every one of the brain-friendly practices. That would be cumbersome and is not necessary. Yet each lesson should be based on many of these aspects of human nature, and in the aggregate, your lessons should incorporate all of them—often. If you are not inclined toward using some of the brain-friendly approaches in your teaching, intentionally find simple ways to work them in. If you don't like to sing or can't play an instrument, use a CD.

REFLECTION: SECOND GRADE

Today I taught the lesson you would have observed Monday, which was creating a model of the solar system using candy. Here's what went well: I explained detailed directions and expectations as well as possible BEFORE we started. Also, their (nearly) finished products look fantastic and I think they'll be proud to show them off for open house.

It became obvious very quickly that they've never been given the opportunity to do something as creative as work with candy. There was lots of talking throughout the lesson. Thankfully, it wasn't any kind of lecture lesson. However, we agreed beforehand that we'd do the steps one at a time, together as a class. I couldn't tell if they were talking about what they were doing during the project, or if it was just 2nd-grade chatter, or bickering, but the noise level was up there and I had to use a bell (the kind you'd see at a post office next to an old index card that used to read "RING FOR SERVICE") to get them to quiet down several times.

It made me wonder, what kind of noise level IS acceptable during this type of lesson. I can guarantee it wouldn't have been anything like this if it was a plain old math program lesson, but by the same token, maybe they couldn't handle the expectations of working with something fun like candy because they don't get to do things like this often.

Or maybe candy is just too naturally tempting for young children to treat as instructional materials! These are all good questions that recognize the reality that some behaviors are just natural and to be expected. Skilled teachers can recognize the difference between the sounds of students actively engaged in their learning and the noise of fooling around.

REFLECTION: FOURTH GRADE

I have to admit that today's science lesson turned out to draw the most enthusiasm from the students. I began the lesson with an introduction to the life cycle of frogs. I received tremendous feedback from the students as I asked questions. They all seem to love learning about animals and the processes they go through.

As I look back on today's lesson I would have to say that the activity that I chose to use turned out to be a tremendous choice. Each student made a life cycle wheel of the frog. I had created one of my own the night before as a model for the students. I did not use the same animal as the one I would have the students construct, in order for them to form their own ideas. It was such a great feeling to see all the students working so intently on their wheels. I realized that the students who are usually falling behind during most lessons kept right up today. The motivation was apparent in the manner in which they attacked this project. I went around and asked questions about the different stages and received correct answers from almost everyone that I questioned. It allowed me to assess them when they were completely unaware of it!

One factor that I need to work on for this lesson and all lessons is enforcing the rule that students are not to shout out during a lesson. I thought the issue had been addressed sufficiently until it became apparent that students felt if their arm was up they could still call out my name in order to get my attention. I have to figure out a way to reconcile this issue.

I am having a great time with science and I always wish there was more time in the day to complete all the great activities that I want to do with the students. I have come to realize that hands-on activities when relating to the subject at hand are such a great asset.

THE CYCLE

Along with Glasser's ideas that all behavior is a search for fulfillment of basic human needs, I especially love the simplicity and elegance that Bernice McCarthy's 4MAT Learning System offers to teachers trying to meet the needs of their students. In *About Learning* she presents a model of the natural learning cycle, four quadrants that represent the logical progression a learner makes from "personal meaning, to expert knowledge, to practical tinkering, and individual creativity" (McCarthy, 2000, p. 202).

The implications for teaching are clear. The 4MAT System takes into account students' learning preferences and how individuals, although they need to participate fully in each part of this cycle, are instinctively drawn to one of the four quadrants. Learning experiences must mimic the natural cycle so every student, no matter her learning style or preference for feeling, thinking, doing, or imagining, can actively connect with the content. The more experience a student has with each phase of the learning process, the more comfortable he becomes participating in all four aspects.

The 4MAT Learning Cycle is comparable to the design of a lesson plan and provides the rationale for why successful instructional lessons follow this basic progression:

- An introduction that is motivating with a connection that is meaningful
- Time spent accruing knowledge and building concepts (the direct instruction and information-gathering phase)
- An opportunity for students to try out what they have just learned (hands-on guided practice and experimentation)
- An evaluation that asks students to demonstrate what they have learned and apply it to new situations (independent practice, closure, and extension activities)

The tenets of the 4MAT System support the Essential Understandings explored in this book. Both incorporate what we know about how the brain works, human motivation, and learning styles into a working framework

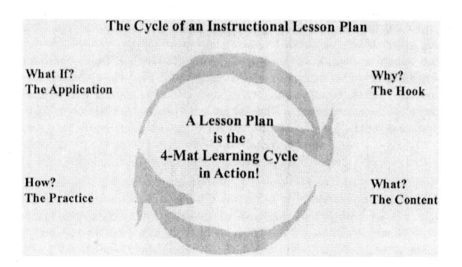

The Cycle of an Instructional Lesson Plan

What If?
The Application

Why?
The Hook

A Lesson Plan
is the
4-Mat Learning Cycle
in Action!

How?
The Practice

What?
The Content

meant to be internalized, to become part of your belief system, and to drive your everyday practice. Here is a summary of the 4MAT Learning Cycle:

Quadrant 1 answers the question *why* by helping students make personal connections. Strategy: Let the students find a reason to want to learn the concepts and material in the first place.

Quadrant 2 answers the question *what* by providing the necessary tools. Strategy: Give students the opportunity to learn the content and develop concepts and understandings.

Quadrant 3 answers the question *how* by giving students the chance to act. Strategy: Provide students with the time to apply and experiment with these concepts and knowledge.

Quadrant 4 answers the question *what if* by encouraging students to think and dream. Strategy: Allow students the opportunity to creatively extend their learning beyond what has been covered.

The 4MAT Learning Cycle clarifies what we know about how people learn. Rather than adding to the stress already felt by beginning teachers who have so much to process and practice in a compacted period of time, it provides a simple framework for our thinking and teaching. You might have already committed the cycle to memory: *Why? What? How? What if?*

Thinking Activity: Evaluating a Lesson for "Brain-Friendliness"

Find an instructional lesson plan from the Internet, a resource book, or a colleague, or choose one you developed yourself. Analyze it for brain-friendliness using the structure of the learning cycle and the "brain loves" list. Does the lesson have a motivating opening, an opportunity to gather expertise, the chance to practice and experiment, and a closure that ties the learning experience together and lets students apply and expand on what they have learned? Which brain-friendly strategies does it incorporate and how do these approaches enhance or limit the learning experience? What would you change or add?

Teachers get their lessons off to a good start and successfully wrap them up by recognizing two *musts* to include in every lesson: a *hook* and a *closure*. The two are critical components of the natural learning cycle and, just as your learner objectives and instructional materials, they deserve to be thought about beforehand and written down in your lesson plan. They are too important to be left to chance. Here is a closer look at how to successfully begin and end a lesson.

THE HOOK

Make sure each lesson has an opening that hooks the students! A motivating introduction catches the brain's interest and gives the students a reason to focus and learn. It provides the "why." So, before you ask students to pay attention and get involved . . .

- Do or say something unexpected.
- Have the students *do* something.
- Use a prop.
- Play music.
- Put on a hat or other piece of clothing.
- Tell a story, sing a song, dance.
- Relate it to prior learning or their lives.
- Pose an open-ended question or puzzle.
- Move the students to a different part of the room.
- Pass out manipulatives.
- Get everyone talking and doing!

It could be something as simple as the personal story the teacher below shared or a song one of my teachers sang about the Underground Railroad. They both helped to get and keep the students' attention. They were hooked to see more.

REFLECTION: SIXTH GRADE

My cooperating teacher was absent today because she had to grade the ELA examinations at the high school. I taught a math lesson in the morning on comparing and ordering fractions. I told the students a story to open up the lesson to try to get their attention. First I told them about how when I was younger I would order my baseball card collection by team order and by position order. The reason that I did that was to make it easier to find what I was looking for because of the order that each card was in.

I also told a brief story about how my brother and I are always being compared by everyone because of all the similarities that we share. These stories worked well to introduce the lesson because it created a brief discussion amongst the students and me about how they order and compare different objects. Overall, I believe this lesson went well, because the students stayed focused from the very beginning of the lesson and they were able to answer the questions that I asked. Also, as I was observing the students do the problems that I assigned them for class work they were able to complete them with ease. During the lesson I felt slightly flustered. Thinking back, I'm not sure it was so bad.

When considering how to hook your students, think what would work best given the time available. Hooks do not all need to be something that takes five minutes out of your lesson. A hook can be a quick attention-getter such as turning off the lights and whispering for the children to get up and silently follow you to the rug. Or it could be a provocative sentence written on the board that startles them, such as, "Starting today, I have a new title—*Queen*—and you must treat me like royalty!" When they walk in and see this on the board, you grab their attention, guaranteed.

THE WRAP-UP

As you wind down the lesson and prepare to move on to something else, make sure you give the lesson a distinct closure. A brief summary solidifies the learning in the brain and lets you assess whether the students know and can demonstrate they learned the main concepts, information, and skills stated in your objectives. It provides the "what if" that allows them a chance to apply what they've learned in a creative way. So, before you move on to something else, tie it all together. Have your students respond, discuss, write, share . . .

- An example of what they learned
- What interested them the most
- Something they were surprised about
- What they will share with their family that night
- The best part of the lesson and why
- Something they want to learn more about

Extend their understanding by asking them to apply this learning to new situations. Then pique their interest by letting them know, in an intriguing way, what they can look forward to next time.

Now get ready to stick up for yourself in Essential Understanding 10!

You Must Have a Reason
For Everything You Do:
If You Cannot Justify It, Don't Do It

STICK UP FOR YOURSELF

Why did you do that? What were you thinking? Once again, this Essential Understanding may just sound like common sense, but being able to stick up for your choices is a necessary part of the job. It is not usually at the forefront of most teachers' minds on any given day, yet it is not an aspect of teaching you can afford to leave to chance. You must be continually mindful and wise about what you say, do, and use when teaching.

REFLECTION: FIFTH GRADE

It is sad getting ready to leave. Today I went to every class with my students. I followed them to math and science and we finished our gingerbread houses. It is fun to go around and see what else they do in school. I have been so wrapped up in social studies, but I see they have a lot to do in math and science as well. It's funny because I remember every peer in high school and college complaining saying, "Does this teacher think this is my only class?" (This was in response to frustration over too much homework from one teacher.)

It made me open my eyes and see how much they have to do. Teaching one subject makes you think your subject is the most important. I never gave my kids that much homework but they did take a bunch of notes and on a day or two I found out they had to take notes in every class. That must not have been fun. In my defense, they are preparing for middle school (too bad MS is focused on taking notes instead of more active learning) but still, the teachers should maybe discuss their plans more. I wish I had taken more time to see what the other teachers were doing each day.

This student teacher gathered information that shed light on what students were being asked to do for homework, and in the process presented a justification for why departmentalized teams benefit from co-planning. For example, in addition to being aware of and reasonable about the students' workload, think how the various team members could integrate their subjects and make assignments meaningful and at a high thinking level.

Students need to be taught in a way that fosters connections—something I call the Velcro approach. Ascertain what is already in the students' heads, what they've been taught, what's going on in their world and in their lives, and picture this as one half of the Velcro fastener. Now throw them a learning experience, the other half of the Velcro fastener that attaches to this background. With nothing to connect to and no motivation to learn or commit it to long-term memory, the brain discards it as irrelevant. Tailor your teaching so that it has something to stick to. This requires conscious thought, decision making, and planning.

COMPETITION: WHY DO WE DO IT?

Parents, teachers, and coaches say children love competition. It does look like the children are having fun. Many children seem to enjoy it when they participate in a sport, play a board game, and race each other. They are also drawn to comparing grades, their lunches, and clothes. Does everyone enjoy this, though? A climate of competition may be fine for the athletic field or as family entertainment. These are organized recreational activities and the participants self-select.

The more difficult task is explaining the purpose and benefits of competition, contests, and reward systems in a classroom and on the playground. We should ask ourselves what it does to risk taking (the basis for learning) and self-confidence. The answers depend on which side you wind up on, the winning or the losing, and whether you are confident or unsure of your skills. They also depend on your individual temperament, whether you are socially outgoing or introverted, whether you think better by yourself with no pressure, whether you do or do not like to have an audience, and what has happened to you in the past in competitive situations.

As you set out to establish the kind of classroom climate children need, decide whether you believe it is important to win and lose, or to learn and work collaboratively. Think about how this belief fits with your goal for students to take risks and to preserve their dignity.

Imagine the effect on morale and relationships if, at a student teaching seminar or faculty meeting, you were made to compete for a prize to see who had taught the *best* lesson that week. Consider what it would feel like if praise were lavished on one teacher and that teacher were held up as a role model, while the rest of you looked on.

Often we blame the students for getting too wound up or for fighting during review games, during spelling bees, or when playing *around-the-world*—when we actually set them up for this kind of behavior. To play around-the-world one student stands next to the student at the next desk (the challenger). The teacher presents them with a question or flashcard. The first student to answer correctly gets to move on to the next challenger and so on until they lose. When the challenger wins, she starts going around the world. It is an exciting and nerve-wracking activity. The student who processes slowly or who is anxious performing in front of a group will likely not perform to his best. Winners and losers are both deeply affected by competition. Both outcomes bring them to a heightened emotional state. We get them excited and get their adrenaline flowing, and then get angry when they "lose it."

So what should teachers do about competition in the classroom? Try this litmus test: If you can't justify a competitive activity as meeting an academic objective or it isn't meeting your classroom climate objectives, then do something else. How about collaboration?

This is what it means to be reflective and to take charge of your classroom, to ensure that whatever you choose to do or say is in harmony with your belief system and instructional goals.

Thinking Activity: From Competition to Collaboration

Your objective is for students to be able to quickly recall the multiplication facts. Keeping your objective in mind, take a competitive math activity such as around-the-world and change it so the activity is fun, collaborative, and mindful of students' needs, motivations, and temperaments.

THE LEGAL TEST

My education law class taught us that teachers must be able to defend their choice of the instructional materials they use with students, and be able to demonstrate that the materials can pass this two-pronged test:

- The materials are age appropriate.
- The materials are relevant to the curriculum.

REFLECTION: THIRD GRADE

This was a great unit! I had so much fun with it! There were so many ways to incorporate external resources such as: books, props, technology, guest speakers, and arts. The students all did very well on the test, which showed me that not only did we get out of our seats and learn in a fun way, but also they learned it all.

When I made up the final test I asked myself if it was too challenging. It was all fill-in. I reviewed it several times, though, and the students did not let me down! What a great reflection on my teaching! I felt very good about myself as I was grading them. I felt that I had done something good for the students.

Yes, straightforward, commonsense criteria. The key is to make a conscious effort to adhere to these criteria, along with your school and district guidelines. You are then on firm ground if your choice of instructional materials or use of classroom time is ever questioned.

A good example of where the two-pronged test should be applied is when choosing a video to show the students. If a movie does not meet these standards it is not a wise or legitimate use of instructional time. Any video, movie, or website you choose to use should be part of a well-thought-out lesson plan or unit, the recommended viewer age should match the age and developmental level of your students, and the students should be held accountable in some way for what they watch.

SORRY, THAT'S CONFIDENTIAL

You also must justify your behavior when it comes to maintaining your students' right to privacy. Keep this in mind when correcting and distributing tests, report cards, and any other papers that have been assessed or graded. Never post grades or have students grade each other's work. Instead of writing the names of students missing their homework on the board, write them on a sheet of paper on your desk or put a sticky-note reminder on the child's desk. Your belief system and an understanding that we all have a basic right to privacy should tell you school is no place for a breach in privacy and public humiliation.

The privacy issue extends to student records. Records are valuable resources physically entrusted to the staff of the school. They are also confidential and are to be used within certain strict legal guidelines. FERPA (the Family Educational Rights and Privacy Act, also known as the Buckley Amendment) is federal legislation that protects students' privacy and upholds parents' rights to see their children's school records.

The prevailing guideline is that a teacher has a right to seek and share information about their students on a need-to-know basis. As a classroom teacher you have access to such information as it relates to your students. There must be a legitimate educational reason for someone to read, share, and discuss the information contained in school records. If you consider how you would want personal information about you or your child handled, it makes perfect sense.

In the case of Individual Education Programs (IEPs), student teachers have the same legal rights and educational responsibilities as the regular classroom teacher. Since you are legally responsible for following the academic and behavioral goals and objectives of the IEP, you have an obligation to read and refer to it. Ask your cooperating teacher, special education consultant, or principal if any classified students are in the class and, if so, make arrangements to read their IEPs.

This is where your discretion and good judgment factor in. Once you have this information, you must keep it confidential; in fact, IEPs must be kept in a locked cabinet or other controlled location. As a beginning teacher, if you are not sure with whom you may share the information and what the protocol is for your particular school, always confer with a supervisor. Follow your school's policies and procedures for keeping records confidential.

For instance, if the physical education teacher asks about the behavior of one of your students and questions whether the IEP behavioral plan offers any suggestions, that teacher has a legitimate right to know. She passes the need-to-know test because she teaches the child and is legally bound to follow the IEP, just as you are. Alternately, if a parent playground volunteer asks the same question, politely refer him to your cooperating teacher or the principal. Decisions about when and why to share such information are handled on a case-by-case basis. Remember that you need to be able to justify everything you do in your role as a teacher, so err on the side of cautious discretion and make good use of your supervisors.

MOTIVES AND DECISIONS

Why we choose to do or say something is our motive. An example of this is in Essential Understanding 7, where we looked at how to use class meetings to teach pro-social skills and solve problems together. To keep with the spirit of the class meeting, your motives for the meetings should be pure. Do not make the mistake of using class meetings or problem-solving strategies as a sugarcoated way to boss your students or discipline certain students. The class meeting becomes your forum, not theirs as intended. They see right through dishonesty and you lose their trust. Also, individual issues are not suitable for a class meeting discussion and should be handled with the student in private, as we previously discussed.

Each day in school you make hundreds of professional decisions. With a belief system to guide you, your instincts help you navigate the bombardment with confidence. When in doubt as to what to do—even a small nagging doubt—hold off on doing anything and ask a colleague or supervisor for help. Sometimes you need to make a split-second decision, such as when one child hits another. It is reasonable and expected that you deal with the misbehavior immediately to keep your students from getting hurt, and then do the problem-solving portion of positive discipline after everyone has calmed down. With less time-sensitive situations such as a parent complaint, choosing a literature book to read to the class, or creating a learning activity, the best thing is to do nothing at all until you've had time to think it through and get guidance. Time and reflection bring wisdom and lead to justifiable choices.

To summarize, you need to be able to justify everything you say and do: curriculum content, materials, books, discipline strategies, choice of words, what you tell others, and so on. This kind of justification is not the same as offering an excuse. Justification is a well-thought-out and genuine reason for your choice. The true reason (motive) that lies behind your choice of behavior and words is found only in your own heart and mind; your choices are out there for all to see and question. When you can justify your choices, you act as a professional who thinks about and works through your actions. This is especially true in how you communicate.

Communication Is the Basis of Relationships: Choose Your Words Wisely

WHAT DID YOU SAY?

Teaching is a highly visible profession. You are in the public eye and always on duty as a representative of your school and the teaching profession. So once again, if you can't justify it, don't say, write, or do it! If you want respect and cooperation from parents, and to be an exemplary role model for your students, write, speak, and act like you are educated, wise, have integrity, and are thoughtful. Model what you expect.

The goal of communication is to understand and be understood. It includes spoken and written words, what you say, how you say it, the motive behind it, what you leave between the lines, and physical communication such as body language and facial expressions. You do not want to be misunderstood, or to express opinions or biases that will undermine the trust you have with students and parents. To make sure this breach does not happen, you need to be careful about what you say.

I recall a teacher who had a rather blunt way of talking about her students. It was not unlike her to write a note home to parents telling them their child was a spoiled brat. Not only is that kind of language inflammatory and unprofessional, it also did little to convey the problem and nothing to establish a rapport with parents and move everyone forward to a solution.

Most parents would be angry if they received a note like that, or if they sat at a parent/teacher conference and had a teacher tell them their child was selfish, stubborn, or lazy. We wouldn't want to hear such hurtful language from our own supervisors or principal. It would not foster a feeling of trust between the two parties. You get what you give, so if you go on the offensive like this, your target will likely react defensively. The battle lines are then drawn and heels dug in.

Communication is at the core of these twelve Essential Understandings. What you do, say, and write is a window into your attitudes and how you view your job, the school, students, and parents. Communications establish your reputation as a teacher and directly impact your teaching success and satisfaction. A cynical view of students can give parents the message that you have given up or that you believe they have ruined their children by not raising them well. It also says you would rather name-call, finger-point, and punish than invest the time and thought necessary to meet your students where they are and to help each child grow in social, emotional, and intellectual skills. Isn't this why you became a teacher in the first place, what you signed on for—to help children have a productive, healthy life?

The antidote to communicating cynicism is to make sure everything you say and write is phrased dispassionately and accurately, in a respectful, constructive, and articulate way—always and everywhere. The goal of your communication about a problem is to objectively describe the behavior while avoiding labeling the child or making judgmental or absolute statements (absolute statements use *always, never, all, none, can't*, and so on).

If a child is having problems concentrating, rather than telling his parents, "He's *always* (an absolute) *lazy* (label) and *daydreams* (judgment) *whenever* (an absolute) he should be working," tell them, "He frequently sits and stares out the window during independent work time and often has work left when the period is over" (objective observation). This statement is right to the point with no labeling or passing of judgment. It conveys the message: This is the situation, it is not acceptable, and now we have to do something about it.

If a student is having a problem working in a cooperative group, rather than saying, "She always bosses the other kids and is obnoxious," say, "She tends to take over the group without asking what the other children think. This causes the other children to not want her on their team." The problem is conveyed in a way that the focus is on the child's choices and behavior, not on her character or her upbringing. It leaves a window of hope that with a concerted intervention and teamwork, you and the parents will find a way to help the child do better.

Thinking Activity: Hmm . . . Let Me Try That Again

Use what you know about empathy to change these comments from inappropriate to appropriate:

She is always butting in line and the others kids don't like her.
The work is too hard for him. He just doesn't "get it."

Every time I ask him to do something he gives me a wise answer and a snotty look.

I'm tired of telling her to sit down and be quiet. She is a pain during lessons.

GROWN-UPS, TOO

This advice also applies to how you communicate with your colleagues and administrators. We know every school has its own culture with norms for behavior. Principals are busy people and have different management and leadership styles. In one school, a principal may encourage teachers to stop by anytime to talk, while in another the principal might prefer you set up an appointment so she can give you her undivided attention. You learn the system for communicating that is particular to that school. This uniqueness of culture holds true in each of your student teaching placements and whenever, throughout your teaching career, you change schools. One thing you can count on: Each school *is* unique.

The approach to discipline at one school might focus on teaching children how to be respectful, responsible members of the community through a working code of conduct, problem-solving strategies, and making reparations. Another school might have more of a rule/consequences, principal's office approach, with frequent use of time-outs and in-school suspensions. Another might leave the approach up to individual teachers. Your success depends on your ability to size up the situation, learn the system, and adapt to working and communicating within the written and unwritten policies and nuances of the school culture. This includes wise choices of whom to go to for guidance, and choosing how and with whom to complain/vent.

REFLECTION: FOURTH GRADE

OK, now they're slowly beginning to open up. I've been taking charge and speaking up so that they start to get used to my voice. My cooperating teacher and I have started to make plans for next week, and I'm teaching my first lesson tomorrow.

Today there was more tension between the teachers. There was a disagreement, and some people seemed to be "backed into corners." I hope this doesn't continue. I think next week I may start to eat in the classroom and do some work. We shall see though. Thank goodness for the other student being there too!!

PROFESSIONAL COMMUNICATIONS

This student teacher was struggling to work within the existing culture. Communications within a school are highly dependent on individuals and what is accepted as "okay" behavior. One of the most important judgment calls you make as a teacher is whether to participate in interpersonal disputes or negative thinking. You need to be able to justify what you say and do.

It helps to remember our previous discussion of the definition of professional teacher conduct and FERPA, the law that protects students' and families' right to privacy. It applies to your non-teaching time as well. With FERPA in mind, try out the staff lounge and decide if you want to eat lunch there, with a smaller group of your colleagues somewhere else, or in your own room. You may be blessed with an upbeat staff room climate where you can use your time to mentally unwind, talk with other adults, and have a few laughs. What you do *not* want is to be drawn into or contribute to an inappropriate discussion of certain parents or children. This is not the way to show you believe teaching is a sacred privilege.

Hopefully your belief system and gut instincts tell you when the conversation has crossed a line. That is your cue to politely excuse yourself and go back to your classroom to peacefully prepare for your afternoon lessons. It is the same with casual conversations in the hall, where Murphy's Law is usually in effect. Count on the reality that you *will* be overheard and what you say *will* be repeated. This is how schools work. They are like small towns in this regard, where you need to consciously work to stay above reproach and protect your reputation. So take the high road and give students, their families, and your coworkers the benefit of the doubt, respect, and privacy you would want for yourself.

Bottom line: Watch what you say and where you say it. This includes e-mail. If you wouldn't want it posted on the bulletin board, don't write it. If you wouldn't want it repeated to your principal, don't say it.

REFLECTION: SIXTH GRADE

Today I learned about being flexible with my schedule. In ELA the reading groups ran long so I didn't have enough time to do one of the activities. I was going to do it tomorrow, but then we were figuring out how many kids would be gone tomorrow for "Take Your Child to Work Day." We realized a lot of kids would be gone so we decided it would be pointless to teach anything important. Then I was going to do the activity on Friday, but we decided to do reading groups and then go to the book fair on Friday. So now I have to fit the activities for this week as well as next week into next week's schedule. I'm going to have to pick and choose to make sure everything that needs to be done gets done. Also, writing in pencil in your planner helps a lot.

Glitches that affect our plans are common. How you respond to these situations communicates your professionalism and work ethic. By being flexible, punctual, enthusiastic, cooperative, open to new ideas and coaching, and by dressing in a way that conveys respect for your position, you communicate how you view you job. While this teacher, like any teacher, did not like the interruptions to the academic day, she took it in stride and showed she had a mature attitude as she worked for a solution. Instead of complaining, she communicated her professionalism and levelheadedness by responding to a trying situation in a calm, thoughtful manner.

THE PROOF IS IN THE READING

Also critical is your ability to communicate your professionalism and intellectual abilities through writing. There is a host of reasons to write: letters to parents, report card comments, curriculum proposals, activity sheets, study guides, a classroom newsletter. The challenge is to make sure that whatever you write is articulate and respectful, and that grammar and spelling are accurate.

The following are some helpful tips for writing professional communications that are of the highest quality. Before you send that note home or make that call, always run it by a trusted colleague or the principal (if that is the norm in your school). Describe the incident honestly using calm, non-inflammatory words and ask for the parent's cooperation. As mentioned in Essential Understanding 4 on home-school relationships, keep good records of your communications so you can refer to specific dates and incidents, and make a copy before you send anything home.

If you send a homework assignment, note, or newsletter home with grammatical or spelling errors, you lose your credibility as someone intelligent and educated enough to be teaching. You also take the risk that a parent return the paper to you—with mistakes corrected! You are a role model, so every time you say or write something incorrectly, you are teaching it incorrectly to your students. I have worked with many beginning teachers who make written and verbal grammatical errors. Sometimes it is through carelessness, while others are not aware that what they are saying is wrong and are surprised when it is pointed out to them. After years of hearing and using certain speech patterns, they have to retrain their ears to make the change. With a positive attitude from the supervisor and a determination to self-correct, it can be done. I have seen it happen. You do not want your message to be lost because of the way it is delivered.

Here are some common communication errors I have identified over the years. These errors are not earth shattering, but being aware of them will help you avoid some common pitfalls and challenges to your competency, as you communicate with others and teach your students.

- Lessons "go *well.*" Lessons do not "go *good.*" Rule of thumb: You do something *well.*
- *A lot* is two words. There is no such word as *alot!*
- *Its* is the possessive form of *it.* Example: The dog lost *its* collar. No apostrophe!
- *It's* is the contraction form of *it is.* Example: *It's* so beautiful out that I hate being stuck inside. This *it's* gets an apostrophe.
- *Aide* is the person; *aid* is another word for *help* (noun) or *to help* (verb).
- Make sure your sentences have both a subject and verb. If not, you are writing *incomplete* sentences, something we teach our students not to do! Incomplete: *Also the book that I borrowed from the library on Native Americans.* What about the book? This is an example of a subject with no predicate. Complete sentence: *The book that I borrowed from the library on Native Americans also got lost somewhere in the classroom.* Ah, now we know what happened to the book!
- Say and write: The *teacher and I spoke* with the students. Do not say or write: The *teacher and me talked* to the students. You wouldn't say *me spoke* with the students!
- Also correct: The principal *spoke to the bus driver and me,* not the *bus driver and I.* Read the sentence with just the *I or me* and see if it sounds right. *I* serves as the subject and *me* as the object.
- Content areas are not capitalized unless they are a language: English, Spanish, social studies, math.
- Avoid the use of multiple exclamation points and emoticons such as *This is going to be such fun!!!* or *Our class picnic was rained out.* :(You can express your enthusiasm with just one exclamation point or a period and it looks more professional.
- Make your verbs agree with plural and singular subjects. Say, The papers *are* going to be graded today, not The papers *is* going to be graded today. Say, *There're* (there are) fifteen days until our class play, not, *There's* (there is) fifteen days. . .
- *The principal is your pal* is a good way to remember which principal/principle to use when writing about the leader of a school.
- Look it up if you aren't sure.
- Use spell/grammar check on everything you write, even e-mail.
- Find some trusted proofreaders and make good use of them.
- Write in straightforward language, free of teacher jargon, that is mindful of the reader.
- Model what you expect from others!

When it comes to communication, teaching gives you a major side benefit. As you teach your students, you also learn and improve. Teaching requires you have a thorough understanding of oral and written language, concepts, content, and skills before you teach them. During student teaching and in your first years in the classroom, you are learning the curriculum at a breakneck pace, often staying just a few chapters or topics ahead of the children. As you become submerged in your preparation to teach, you are taking crash courses in a variety of topics and skills.

Teaching English Language Arts (ELA) improves your speaking and writing skills. Holding class meetings teaches you the language of respect and the ability to actively listen and respond thoughtfully. Encouraging empathy from your students helps you be empathetic to them, their parents, and your school coworkers. You learn to choose your words carefully. An added benefit? These new proficiencies also transfer over to your personal life. You become a better communicator in all aspects of your personal and professional life, and, as our final essential understanding stresses, you learn how to talk with yourself as you reflect on everything you do and say.

Essential Understanding 12

Reflection Is the Key
to Your Continued Growth:
Do It Regularly With Honesty

A FAVORITE QUOTE

If there is anything that we wish to change in the child, we should first examine it and see whether it is not something that could be better changed in ourselves.

—Carl Gustav Jung

This Carl Jung quote is a well-articulated description of the goal of self-evaluation for teachers and parents. If you are to grow, in teaching as in your life, continually ask yourself how things are going, how you feel about what is happening, and why. And you have to understand what role you played in the situation. It does not matter if the outcome was a positive one or a negative one; the key is to be able to replicate or avoid the result in the future.

ASK *WHAT* AND *WHY,* AND THEN *REPLICATE* OR *AVOID*

It is common to focus on the negative. Many beginning teachers have an easier time identifying and explaining what went wrong than explaining why something went well. In the spirit of asset-building, our goal is the development of awareness of positive behaviors that successfully help us meet our goals. You can only consciously repeat that which you have identified—otherwise it is hit or miss.

If you are playing softball in the outfield and you catch more fly balls when you wear your sunglasses, then you want to consciously wear those sunglasses the next time. And if you give an independent math assignment and

---

REFLECTION: FIFTH GRADE

Today something dawned on me that is probably so obvious to you! If you know your students, you should/could tailor your lesson plans to their individual personalities. Taking into account habits and situations of students will provide the teacher with a way to avoid unnecessary hassles and delays. For instance J. is in my reading group and as his teacher says, "J. will do things the way J. wants to do them." I have found that no matter how explicitly I go over directions, he always does it differently. So, today, I stood behind him while the students started and directed him (twice) when he started to do something differently. If I had done this earlier, I wouldn't have had to hand back assignments to be corrected.

---

discover the students follow the procedure more accurately when the steps are posted 1, 2, and 3 on the board, then you want to consciously post the steps the next time. Or if you are unhappy with the way the students speak to each other, examine how you speak to them.

THAT IS WHAT YOU ARE HERE FOR

A daily habit of mind of self-reflection and openness to new ideas—both large and small—is the way to mature into the teacher you strive to be, one who never rests on her laurels or becomes cynical.

Most of your growth as a beginning teacher comes through external sources and self-evaluation, and from what you do with the feedback you receive from your supervisors and students. As you progress as a teacher, receive tenure, and finish your education degrees, you are not as closely supervised. You have successfully made it through the probation period and done well enough to be trusted to continue as a teacher. This is why it is so important that you become a self-motivated, reflective practitioner, one who challenges himself to continually grow and improve, tenure or not, no matter who is watching, no matter how many years you have been teaching.

Once again, attitude is everything, especially how you take constructive feedback. Your beginning teaching experiences are rewarding when you take feedback willingly, with an open mind—and even beyond that, when you *actively seek* it. Part of the equation is to take advantage of opportunities to learn, reflect, and apply. Be a sponge for knowledge when you attend faculty meetings, in-service trainings, open houses, curriculum nights, school events, and parent conferences.

Workshops, especially those teachers are required to attend, have not requested, and have no choice in designing, often elicit grumbling; teachers would rather use the time working in their classroom or teaching their students. But when you view these as opportunities, in-service training can be eye opening. Even when the training seems to be just more of what you already know, with an open mind you can take home something of value from every experience. Often, that one tip or idea makes the whole experience worthwhile. As the reflection below illustrates, your increasing insight and skill set gives you a solid foundation that helps you anticipate and plan for what might happen when working with children.

REFLECTION: THIRD GRADE

In order to prepare for the unit test I decided to pass out a review sheet that modeled some of the questions that would be on the test. Before passing out the sheets I gave the necessary directions and asked the students to begin working. This was to be an independent activity, the first that I had given. Most of my other lessons were direct instruction but I decided to let the students do their own investigating. They were able to use their books and their notes. The sheet was a simple true/false review where the students had to change the false answers to make them true. Overall, I think the review sheet was a good idea. It made the students responsible for their own learning.

However, there were a few students who kind of missed the boat on this activity. I should have known that they would as they have limited attention spans and motivation when working on their own. Later in the week, after attending the seminar on meeting the needs of diverse students, it occurred to me that perhaps I should have set up some sort of alternative scenario for these students. In the future I will take their diverse needs into consideration in order to make sure that everyone benefits.

SELF-REFLECTION CAN BE TAUGHT

Cognitive refers to conscious intellectual activity such as thinking, reasoning, or remembering, and *coaching* is when you train intensively as by instruction and demonstration. Combined they become *cognitive coaching*, an approach to supervision where mentors lead their teachers to practice rigorous self-evaluation, all the time, even when not being observed or being asked.

The purpose of cognitive coaching is to walk teachers through the analytical process of self-discovery by training them to ask themselves what went well and why, and what did not go well and why, and to identify what to do differently next time. Applying the new understanding in the classroom is the practical part of this process, the aspect that makes metacognition more than a purely intellectual pursuit. The key is finding connections between what you did and what your students did. Identify the unsuccessful choices and remove them from your teaching repertoire. Identify the successful behaviors and make them an integral part of your repertoire. Integrate them with your belief system, and go into your next teaching situation armed with concrete, cognitively based strategies. This approach can be applied to any interactions you have with your students, especially when implementing positive discipline.

ISN'T IT GREAT TO HAVE CHOICES?

We have established that reflective teaching is based on two simple questions—what did or did not go well and why, and what role you played—and that you look inside yourself for answers. Notice the emphasis is on the choices *you, the teacher,* make and *your* behavior. We are back to William Glasser's control theory. Even with all the academic and social issues you have to deal with, never forget that ultimately you are in charge of your teaching. The makeup of the students and the degree of financial and professional support you get from the school and parents are major factors, yet you have a tremendous and almost infinite influence on what happens in your classroom. This is not to imply that it is easy. You cannot simply and unilaterally change who your students are, or secure better funding, yet you can change your approach to working with students and families.

The twelve Essential Understandings are a combination of philosophical processes. *Idealism* involves forming ideals of what should be and living accordingly. *Pragmatism* is thinking about the practical consequences of your beliefs and acting accordingly. In the spirit of *pragmatic idealism*, a cognitive coach views you as a learner, and guides you to try out and test your beliefs in real-life situations, then reassess and tweak them, and apply them again. You can make the ideal happen.

Imagine that you are excited because your students are doing well on their social studies research project. Other teachers at your grade level say this degree of success has not always been the case. The students are including multiple references and are comparing and contrasting views of various authors, even supporting their ideas with details. You are thrilled and share it with your mentor or supervisor (your cognitive coach).

Your mentor asks you what you did to help the students be so successful. You smile proudly and say you don't know. She prods you to recall what you did to prepare the students for the assignment and the materials you used. Ah ha! Now you get it!

You took them to the library media center and had the media specialist show them some excellent sites to use for their research. In ELA and in prior social studies lessons you taught the students how to use Venn diagrams and T-charts to compare and contrast. You also taught them the difference between a fact and an opinion. You gave them a pre-printed study guide to use while doing their Internet research, which helped them record citation information and keep the information they collected from different resources separate from each other. You also helped them choose a topic they were interested in.

Now it is apparent that you did a whole host of things that influenced their success. Once you get accustomed to this way of analyzing your teaching, you discover that you *do* know what makes a successful learning experience after all, and now you can cognitively incorporate your great ideas (beliefs) into your teaching repertoire (behaviors).

This mental process of following your intuition and seeking help from others is critical for good lesson planning. The logical progression from planning and trying things, to reflecting on them, and making determinations about likely causes and effects allows you to anticipate what will happen in the future. The next time your intuition will alert you that you might be off track. With experience comes a core foundation of understandings that serves as a guide for future planning and management decisions. Predicting is not random guessing or making unfounded assumptions; it is based on solid information and understanding of how things work. It requires having a knowledge base and relevant experiences, analyzing them, synthesizing the concepts, evaluating their appropriateness for future actions, and justifying your choices. It is learning from experience, and everything we learn becomes a tool to anticipate

---

REFLECTION: SIXTH GRADE

Going into today, I struggled with what to do in science for a lesson. I went over many different things in my head. There was so much information in the next section to teach, and I wanted to do something else than just stand before the class and do a walk through and discussion of the volcano section of the day. I came in this morning with a plan that I was not so happy with, and I talked about how I was feeling with my cooperating teacher. We discussed how that happens when you are teaching, and we talked about changing it to having the students do science stations around the room on the topic. That was something I never thought of and thought it would be perfect.

I was very comfortable with it. It did not require a lot of extra work to get the stations ready either, because I already had the stuff on hand because I was going to use them anyway, so to separate them into stations was not difficult at all or extra work. It went very well! I think it went better than what I had planned. I am glad I changed my lesson plan to stations.

the future. Soon we internalize what we have discovered and our practice becomes more grounded.

The following scenario is a walk-through of this process.

- The experience provides information (*What happened?*): My second-graders were only able to read half of what I had planned for this afternoon's ELA lesson. They started to talk and fool around with their partner after five minutes. I kept telling them to stop fooling around and they kept at it. I got annoyed and sent them back to their seats and I read it aloud to them as they (hopefully) followed along silently.
- From knowledge comes analysis (*Why did this happen?*): I realized afterward that they were too tired after recess to concentrate; the book was too long and at too difficult a reading level for many of them; the pairs weren't balanced for reading skill levels; they weren't very interested in the topic; I didn't invest enough time in pre-selling the book and setting clear expectations for behavior; and I started to panic when they wouldn't pay attention and I saw we were going to run out of time.
- Analysis of the factors leads to synthesis (*What can I improve on?*): I will choose developmentally appropriate reading materials; I will choose a better time of the day for ELA; I will spend time generating interest in the book and helping students connect it to their lives; I will select buddy reading partners more carefully; I will post and review a written chart of the steps for working on the activity and make sure the children understand before I send them off to read; I will not take it out on the children when the problem is clearly my fault.
- Synthesis leads to evaluation and a well-founded generalization (*How can I make sure this doesn't happen again?*): I will use what I've learned through the experience to anticipate the cause and effect of my choices. When I plan activities I will avoid problems by predicting what my students need and what approaches and materials will work best.

Learning from experience requires a process of higher-level thinking that takes us from what happened to how to do better next time. Benjamin Bloom would be so proud to see his higher-level thinking skills taxonomy in practice.

--- ∞∞∞ ---

Thinking Activity: Let Me Try That

Choose a lesson you have taught to put through the walk-through process. Take a few minutes to answer each of the questions starting with *What happened?* and ending with *How can I make sure this doesn't happen again?*

--- ∞∞∞ ---

NORMS SET EXPECTATIONS

All of this introspection on your part helps you choose your teaching approaches and intentionally set up the classroom climate you want. Now when students walk into your room they know what is expected of them, what is permissible and what isn't. This is true because you are more confident and clear in what you expect and how to make it happen. It may be quite different from what is expected from them in the classroom next door, and they are savvy enough to adjust their behavior accordingly. This is why each of us can make a difference, because we have a circle of influence. These commonly accepted practices and attitudes shared by a community are called *norms*. Norms are what is normal for that setting. Norms create the culture, and your classroom is a mini-culture of your own making.

When you get to your student teaching assignment or when you have your own class, think about the norms in your classroom, in other classrooms, and the school. What do these expectations say about what the administration, faculty, and staff believe about children and education? What do they teach children about what is expected of them? What do they say to parents? Are these the messages you want yourself to give to your students and their families?

Thinking Activity: Conscious and Unconscious Norms

Here are some typical classroom norms to reflect on and evaluate. Ask yourself how you and others handle these situations and determine the messages they send.

- How are class rules determined and by whom?
- How is bullying handled?
- What happens when a new child joins the class?
- How are student conflicts handled?
- What happens when a child breaks a class rule?
- When are children allowed to speak out loud?
- What happens when homework is not completed?
- When are children permitted to get out of their seats?
- How do children line up and walk in the halls?
- What is the procedure for going to the bathroom? Getting a drink?
- What happens when a child is home ill for two days?
- How are partners or cooperative groups chosen?
- How do parents participate in the classroom?

- What is the procedure for collecting and returning students' work?
- How is tattling handled?
- How are students' desks or tables arranged?
- What happens when a special area teacher complains about your class?
- How is appreciation shown for children's efforts?

Keeping in mind that, as a teacher, you must be able to defend everything you do and say, how did you and others fare? You likely found many norms that you are pleased with and some that you now want to change, or avoid instituting when you get your own classroom. Some are worth having, whereas some may be indefensible. Taking stock of your practice and the norms you have established keeps you fresh, and keeps your teaching and classroom climate in line with your beliefs.

The two reflections that follow show one student teacher trying to establish the norm for talking in his class, and another realizing she needs to be more consistent in establishing the norm for proper behavior.

REFLECTION: SIXTH GRADE

I thought today was going to be a normal day of teaching but I was definitely wrong. We had planned to read a section out of the textbook and then demonstrate some of the ideas for the students. After I observed my teacher I was somewhat nervous. She said she had a difficult time teaching the material because the children were not paying attention. I thought she did well teaching the material despite the fact that it was very meaty and there were not a lot of hands-on materials for the students. I decided to try something different and I noticed that it went quite well. The children actually learned something from it and they were interested. The only problem I found was my energy level. I was drained from talking and moving around so much by the end of the second class. It was a good, tired feeling knowing I put my best effort into teaching.

I also tried to keep the students quieter while I was teaching today. It worked just as my teacher had said. When I just stood there and waited, it only took them about 5 seconds to quiet down and look right at me. I also told them I would wait for them to be quiet when they were talking. They quieted down the second I asked them to, which shows me that they actually respect me. It is a good feeling when you have control over your classroom. I thought today was one of those "learning" days because I learned a lot about my students as well as myself.

REFLECTION: SECOND GRADE

My objectives in the lesson were that the students would be able to tell what taste buds are, be able to locate them on a tongue, explain the importance of taste buds, and be able to identify foods correctly as being salty, sweet, sour, or bitter.

It was a good lesson, but there is always room for improvement. Watching the tape, I realized I said the word "ok" far too many times. I need to stop doing that. Also, I could have gone about doing the lesson another way, such as giving them a sheet to fill out where they put an "X' in the columns of the taste for each food, tell where they tasted the food the most on their tongue, and then discussed their answers in a class discussion to conclude the activity instead of me filling out the big chart with them as a group. I would have been freed up to walk around more of the room and to more of the students instead of just walking around to the front of the tables watching and talking to them as I did.

Watching the tape, I saw a couple of students goofing off that I did not notice during the lesson. I have to watch where I am, making sure my back is not turned so mischief can occur. It is hard with a large class and as spread out as they are in my room. I also was caught up in my words a couple times and looked at the chart once. I have to watch this also so that the lesson does not get thrown off.

What excellent examples of helpful reflections! They were a blend of honest analysis and a determination to problem solve for solutions. These students showed they knew that in order to change their behavior or thinking, they had to be able to look critically at themselves. They had an open mind, a good attitude, and the ability to have their work critiqued without feeling threatened. That good attitude made working with them a pleasure.

GOING DEEPER WITH METAPHORS

Another wonderful and infectious way to explore the ultimate nature of a concept is the brain-friendly process of creating metaphors. Mental exercises that ask us to relate one concept to another with figurative language let us reach down into our core and zero in on our true perspectives and beliefs. Metaphors, similes, and analogies can clear our heads and bring us back to the simple essence of an idea. Figurative language makes us slow down and reflect, and therefore stay grounded. This abstract thinking can serve as a welcome alternative to a more linear thinking process. It works beautifully with your students as well as with any subject area.

Think about the concept of mutual respect. We have likely experienced relationships that were based on, and ones that lacked, mutual respect. The essence of a relationship is the respect that members of a partnership or group afford each other. School climate is about the nature of these relationships among members of a school community.

Consider these figurative words of wisdom from a group of my student teachers, responding to the metaphor "Discipline is a house of cards":

No matter how many times it falls, you've got to keep building them up.
High expectations make them fall apart.
When one card falls they all come tumbling down.
When you get frustrated, things get shaky.
It needs a strong foundation.
Sometimes you've got to walk away and come back later.
Complicated structures fall apart easier.
If we had a support system it would make it easier.
Needs repair and maintenance.
Is multifaceted—has many parts.
Some plans don't work, so you develop new plans.

———

Thinking Activity: Let the Simile Bloom

"A relationship is like a flower." Take this simile, preferably in a group or with another teacher, and brainstorm how a relationship and a flower are similar. Let your creative energy wrap itself around the simile and let your ideas emerge. The more time you give yourself to allow one idea to spark another, the deeper and more profound your thinking can go.

———

Share your ideas with each other. If my experience is a guide, I bet you are impressed with the beautiful concepts you and the others came up with. I have never ceased to be amazed at what my students and teachers could do with figurative language. This is a way of stepping back from the mundane to reflect on a deeper level about what is important. You can go a step further and use these metaphors to create belief statements, and you are then on the road to defining a code to live by and the basis for your professional choices.

Reflection is the underpinning of good teaching, and therefore, the basis for happy, successful teachers and students. It is ultimately the underpinning of anything in life that we are dedicated to doing well. As we have said throughout this book, beliefs are what give us direction and drive real change. Without beliefs to guide us, we try anything; we are swayed by the moment and then swallowed up by the system. With clear commitments and goals built on our beliefs and attention on how we are doing, we know when we have been successful and what to aspire to next.

Conclusion:
Final Thoughts

THE ESSENCE

Successful teaching is all about nurturing healthy relationships.

Do all the good you can,

> By all the means you can,
> In all the ways you can,
> In all the places you can,
> At all the times you can,
> To all the people you can,
> As long as you ever can.

—John Wesley, eighteenth-century Anglican clergyman

What a beautiful, poignant message, especially for teachers. With their commonalities, these twelve Essential Understandings underscore how important it is that your classroom be filled with positive energy and that you do all the good you can in your important role of teacher. This is essential and with the right spirit attainable, even if the rest of your world is not quite so optimistic. It takes a conscious effort to maintain a generous, hopeful attitude and be true to your beliefs. The teaching profession is complicated and filled with challenges and disappointments, so it helps to stay mindful of not being drawn into negative thinking. Learn the difference between criticizing versus evaluating, and gossiping versus seeking help from others. It is about having pure motives that show respect for teaching and treat it like a privilege. Your motives drive your choices and determine the eventual outcome of your efforts. Students, parents, and your coworkers can tell if you are sincere and can feel the power of your good intentions.

REFLECTION: FIFTH GRADE

Today was a sad day. I did not think it would be as hard as it was to say good-bye to my students and I did not think they would be as upset as they were. A couple of the girls could not stop crying during the day. Another cooperating teacher and mine planned a pizza party for both of us without us knowing. It was really sweet and meant a lot to me. I did not think they were going to do anything for us. The students loved it and had a great time, even though some of them got emotional (including us).

HAVE I MADE A DIFFERENCE?

When it comes down to it, teachers, as is true with students and their parents, really do not ask for much. They simply want to know they make a difference and are appreciated. Why else would teachers keep a desk drawer filled with thank-you notes from students and parents? Why else would they get so excited when a lesson goes well or a student finally "gets it"? Why else would they spend their own money on materials and come in on the weekends to create classrooms that are inviting and stimulating to their students? And why else would they well up with tears when they send their students home on the last day of school?

These reflections express these simple joys found in the teacher-student relationship.

REFLECTION: FIRST GRADE

Today was the best day of my teaching so far. During math today I realized exactly why I wanted to become a teacher. I prepared a lesson on patterns and how to create them. I let the children explore with patterns the previous day and allowed them to compare their patterns with others. Today, however, I asked them to come up with a few patterns on their own and try to name them. They immediately began naming all the patterns based on color and even yelled out when their pattern looked like someone else's.

The most shocking point of my lesson that put a permanent smile on my face was when I asked them to label their patterns with A's and B's. The children, every single one of them, labeled their pattern correctly. When I held up a few patterns to the class all of the students were able to name the pattern and create one similar to it. This lesson alone made the past few weeks of teaching math worth every second. I couldn't believe how every student was able to create a pattern and then name it with ease. I walked out of the school today smiling and sad. Smiling because I started to think about my past lessons and all of the problems I had, as well as the positives. Sad because a lot of the students realized that I am only going to be here one more week, and they were actually sad I am leaving. I don't want to go to my second placement. I think I am too attached to my 1st graders.

REFLECTION: FIFTH GRADE

First, I want to say thanks for volunteering to be a reference. Hopefully everything will turn out well. My fingers are crossed. Anyway, my cooperating teacher was out today because she was at a meeting for a new reading program, so even though the consultant teacher was still in, it was like a solo day for me. The children exceeded my expectations, as they were very well behaved, especially considering the not-so-normal day we were having. . . . Basically, there was only about an hour of real instruction because of so many activities, but I found it to be pleasing because the students got to relax a little bit and not have such a stressful day. The other 5th grade teachers commented a few times on how well behaved my class was, but I really didn't expect anything else from the students. I can't tell you how excited I am to have my own class—not just to teach content and curriculum, but to start developing a classroom community from the first minute of the school year. I just can't wait.

What genuine, unadulterated joy and love is shown in these reflections. The student teachers were truly inspired and anxious to get into their own classrooms to work their magic. They discovered what good teaching is and felt the power of the emotional bond they can have with students. This deep personal connection is a unique blessing that few other professions enjoy. They are ready to live the life of a teacher, motivated from the inside out, and as their mentor, I could hope for nothing better.

Your belief-driven practice combined with your circle of influence is very powerful, and you just might be the catalyst for an improved school culture. At the minimum, you have a profoundly positive effect on a group of children and their families, and you realize a high level of personal and professional pride and satisfaction that helps you continue on your teaching journey.

IT ALL FITS TOGETHER

The highest level of professionalism in any field of endeavor is born of reflection and a continued quest for information, understanding, and self-knowledge that is initiated of the practitioner's own accord. When we think we have all the answers, we stop learning; we stop seeking the truth. In all matters we are learners first. The passion and commitment to succeed at your mission come from within you, and your integrity never lets you do anything less than what is the best for your students.

Reflect on these twelve Essential Understandings before and during your new teaching experiences. Add new understandings as you think of them. They help you know what you believe and how to create a classroom that intentionally puts your beliefs to work. You then have attitudes and expectations of yourself and others that are lofty and ideal, realistic and attainable. The resulting relationships and sense of hope will get you off to a good start in your teaching career and help sustain you for many years.

Above all, these attitudes and behaviors are a living testament to your belief that teaching is a privilege, and you are living proof that teachers can and do work magic.

Epilogue:
A Classroom Story

This story is a look at the first day of a new school year through the eyes of a child. It expresses all I believe about the nature of the student-teacher relationship. I wrote the story to celebrate that magical place called a classroom, where good things are the norm.

As you read "First Day Magic" to yourself or aloud to your students, think about how Mrs. Morales weaves the twelve Essential Understandings into the everyday workings of her classroom. Are you the kind of teacher Kyle hoped for?

FIRST DAY MAGIC

He thought it would never come yet here it was, finally. It was the letter that would tell him something he couldn't wait another minute to know.

Dear Parents,

We are happy to tell you that your child is in Mrs. Morales's third-grade class this year. Her room number is 17. We look forward to seeing everyone on September 6th. Enjoy the rest of your summer.

Sincerely,
Mrs. Walker, Principal

"Hey, Kyle! Did you get the letter from school?" his friend Paul asked him that afternoon. "I have Mr. Gleason. Who'd you get?"

"I've got Mrs. Morales," Kyle answered. He said it like he knew her, but he didn't. He couldn't even put a face to the name.

———∞∞∞———

That night, as he was drifting off to sleep, Kyle dreamed about this new teacher, this Mrs. Morales. He wondered what she would be like. Would she smile a lot? Would she make them work hard? Would she like him? He would have to wait until September to find out. Kyle did not like meeting new teachers and new kids very much. It seemed like he was doing a lot of that since he moved here last April. It still didn't feel like his school.

———∞∞∞———

As always happens, September followed August. August was freedom and lazy days doing what you wanted. September was school and early mornings out of bed. Kyle was one of the big kids in school now! Third grade!

The first day of school came as expected. Kyle wasn't sure he was ready to face that new teacher, Mrs. Morales. So he sat there, too nervous to eat the bowl of cereal he had poured for himself. The corn crisps swelled with milk as he sat there staring.

"Hurry up, Kyle," his mother warned from the living room. "You'll miss the bus! Wouldn't that be a great way to start a new school year? Late on the first day!"

He still didn't move. He let the cereal get soggier and soggier as the countdown to school continued. He knew that refusing to eat wouldn't stop the countdown. A new school year was about to begin whether he ate his cereal or not. He finally dumped the mess in the garbage and grabbed his backpack off the hook. He reached up to kiss his mother good-bye.

"You be good, now, you hear me? You listen to the teacher and no monkey business!" He nodded in return. "And have a good time," she added with a big hug.

A good time? At school? With a new teacher? No way.

———∞∞∞———

The bus ride was short, only ten minutes. Kyle sat with Paul, wishing that the ride were longer, like an hour or maybe even two. He noticed Paul was quieter than usual. The children slowly stepped off the bus and walked into school. A few of the little kids who had cried as they got on the bus were now silent. Kyle didn't cry, of course, even though he felt like he might if he weren't careful. He didn't want Paul and the other kids to laugh at him.

Some children carried new boxes of crayons and wore new sneakers, just like Kyle. On the outside they looked ready for the new school year. On the inside they had first-day butterflies dancing in their stomachs, just like Kyle. The fluttering made them feel funny.

Kyle and the other children filed down the hallway to find their classrooms. When Kyle got to room 17, he said goodbye to Paul. "See you at lunch."

"I'll save you a seat," Paul promised him. As Kyle turned to go inside the classroom he saw a sign on the door that said, "Welcome to a Magical Place!" He wondered what would be so magical about it. Wasn't this just school?

Slowly Kyle entered the room. His eyes searched wildly to find the teacher. There she was, near the coat hooks. Mrs. Morales was squatting down so low he could hardly find her. She was the size of the children.

Her bright red skirt flowed around her legs like a beautiful parachute. She hunched to the floor while her new children crowded around, watching and listening. They were looking for clues that would tell them what this new teacher was like. Kyle stood off to the side.

Mrs. Morales's voice was clear and gentle as she greeted each of them by name. Her squatting made it easier for her to look the children in the eye as she talked. "You must be Carlena, and you were the first one in the room today! You are an early bird!" I'm an early bird, too, thought Kyle, but she didn't even notice.

"And here come Felicia and Benjamin. You two ride the bus together, don't you?" Kyle knew Benjamin from last year and was glad to see a face he recognized.

"This must be Andrew, who loves baseball so much." How could she know that? Kyle puzzled. He inched closer. Will she ever notice me?

"Kara, come let me see your lovely braids. Who did all this braiding for you?" Mrs. Morales's own dark hair was pulled back behind her ears and held firmly by a giant wooden clip painted with bold colors. Her face was bright and friendly. Large parrot earrings hung from her ears. The children stared as the parrots bobbed and twirled as she talked. Kyle's eyes were glued to the dangling shapes.

"So, what do you think of my crazy earrings?" she asked. "I have birds on my ears! Isn't that a funny place for birds?" The teacher laughed out loud. Her smile reached far across her face, a kind of magic smile that had the power to make smiles appear on the faces of others. Even sad Kyle with the uneaten cereal was touched by her magic. He felt a smile sprout on his own face at her silliness and out came a giggle. Then Mrs. Morales turned toward him and softly rested her hand on his shoulder. "I'm so glad you are in my class this year, Kyle. I heard you like to write stories and so do I! We will be a great team."

Mrs. Morales and me a team? Kyle smiled at the thought. His stomach butterflies began to quiet down.

After Mrs. Morales welcomed each of her new students, she invited them to look around the room. "This is *your* room now. Wander around with a friend and get to know your new home." She found partners for those who had none. Kyle stood waiting. "Mayra, please help Kyle look around the room. Shauna, could you be Lynne's partner? She's new to our school and needs a friend."

Mrs. Morales had spun her special magic on the room as well. It was colorful and full of wonderful things to look at. A soft blue rug was spread out beneath the windows, ready for a circle of children. Kyle rubbed his hand over the blue fibers. A large pad of lined paper hung on the wooden easel. Kyle imagined all the stories he could write on that pad of paper.

A rocking chair sat piled with flowered pillows waiting for a storyteller to climb aboard. Child after child climbed on to try it out. Kyle waited his turn, and then sat down. It felt comfortable and cozy. He didn't want to get up . . . ever. The library shelves stood stacked with books filled with poems and stories and things to learn. Their spines faced out, all in neat rows.

Kyle and Mayra darted here and there. They discovered magnifiers, shells, math cubes, and a large stuffed bear. Then as Kyle walked by the supply shelf his elbow hit a basket of markers. They tumbled out onto the floor making a great clattering noise. His face grew hot. He scrambled to pick them up before anyone noticed, remembering his mother's reminder to stay out of trouble. A hand reached out to help him.

"I did the same thing myself yesterday. Maybe we should move them further back on the shelf." Mrs. Morales smiled as she pushed the basket to the back.

She wasn't mad at him!

Mayra tugged at Kyle's arm and led him to a large bulletin board in the back of the room. The children pointed out their names. "So, you found our Special People Board! Later this morning each of you will draw a picture of yourself to go with your name. But first, there is something waiting for you on the desks. My students from last year left you a surprise."

The desks were pushed together into groups of four. Stuck to the upper right-hand corner was a nametag in the shape of a pencil. The children helped each other find their desks. "Kyle, here's your desk, right next to mine," Benjamin called out. On each desktop was a piece of construction paper, folded in half, standing on its edges like a tent. One side of the construction paper had a picture drawn in crayon and markers. The other side had a carefully written note. The notes started with "Dear Friend." One by one the children read the messages aloud.

"Wait until you see the science corner and the magnets!"

"You'll have class meetings and people really listen to you."

"Do you like to write stories and read fun books? This is the place! You even get to sit in the author's chair."

"Remember to talk out your problems. Mrs. Morales doesn't like fighting."

"We have group time every morning on the blue rug. You get to sing and read poems and talk, and talk, and talk!"

"Don't worry about being bored. There is always something exciting going on here."

"Hey, Kyle. What does yours say?" someone yelled. Kyle read his letter out loud. "You are lucky to be in this class. We have lots of fun. Mrs. Morales is the best teacher you could get." He had already started to figure that out for himself.

As the children talked and read their letters, rectangles of paper hung from the ceiling swaying above their heads. The mobiles carried simple messages. "We are thinkers. We are writers. We are listeners. We are explorers. We are artists. We are readers. We are scientists. We are helpers. We are peacemakers. We are friends."

It looked like this *was* a magical place, just like the sign on the door said. The butterflies were gone now and Kyle was ready—ready to work and play and laugh and think with his new teacher. He couldn't wait to tell his mother about Mrs. Morales when he got home.

Mrs. Morales. Wonderful, magical Mrs. Morales!

RESOURCES

Use this formal written behavioral intervention for problems that are more serious or ongoing. The *teaching* rather than *telling* approach is very effective. For a younger student who may have difficulty writing, have him tell you what he thinks and write it down. Give the child a copy to take home and keep one for yourself. Set a time to check with the student on his progress and remember to follow-through as necessary.

YOU CAN DO BETTER!

Student's Name: _____

Date: _____ Teacher: _____

What behavior got you into this situation? _____

_____

_____

Why was this behavior a problem? _____

_____

_____

What will you choose to do instead next time? _____

_____

_____

Consequence: How will you fix the problem you caused? _____

_____

_____

_____

_____   _____

   Student sign here   Teacher sign here

Note: This document can be reproduced for use in the classroom. It was published in
Elizabeth C. Manvell, *Teaching Is a Privilege: Twelve Essential Understandings for
Beginning Teachers* (Lanham, MD: Rowman & Littlefield Education, 2009).

40 Developmental Assets® for Middle Childhood

Search Institute® has identified the following building blocks of healthy development—known as Developmental Assets®—that help young people grow up healthy, caring, and responsible.

External Assets

Support
1. **Family support**—Family life provides high levels of love and support.
2. **Positive family communication**—Parent(s) and child communicate positively. Child feels comfortable seeking advice and counsel from parent(s).
3. **Other adult relationships**—Child receives support from adults other than her or his parent(s).
4. **Caring neighborhood**—Child experiences caring neighbors.
5. **Caring school climate**—Relationships with teachers and peers provide a caring, encouraging environment.
6. **Parent involvement in schooling**—Parent(s) are actively involved in helping the child succeed in school.

Empowerment
7. **Community values children**—Child feels valued and appreciated by adults in the community.
8. **Children as resources**—Child is included in decisions at home and in the community.
9. **Service to others**—Child has opportunities to help others in the community.
10. **Safety**—Child feels safe at home, at school, and in his or her neighborhood.

Boundaries & Expectations
11. **Family boundaries**—Family has clear and consistent rules and consequences and monitors the child's whereabouts.
12. **School Boundaries**—School provides clear rules and consequences.
13. **Neighborhood boundaries**—Neighbors take responsibility for monitoring the child's behavior.
14. **Adult role models**—Parent(s) and other adults in the child's family, as well as nonfamily adults, model positive, responsible behavior.
15. **Positive peer influence**—Child's closest friends model positive, responsible behavior.
16. **High expectations**—Parent(s) and teachers expect the child to do her or his best at school and in other activities.

Constructive Use of Time
17. **Creative activities**—Child participates in music, art, drama, or creative writing two or more times per week.
18. **Child programs**—Child participates two or more times per week in cocurricular school activities or structured community programs for children..
19. **Religious community**—Child attends religious programs or services one or more times per week.
20. **Time at home**—Child spends some time most days both in high-quality interaction with parents and doing things at home other than watching TV or playing video games.

Internal Assets

Commitment to Learning
21. **Achievement Motivation**—Child is motivated and strives to do well in school.
22. **Learning Engagement**—Child is responsive, attentive, and actively engaged in learning at school and enjoys participating in learning activities outside of school.
23. **Homework**—Child usually hands in homework on time.
24. **Bonding to school**—Child cares about teachers and other adults at school.
25. **Reading for Pleasure**—Child enjoys and engages in reading for fun most days of the week.

Positive Values
26. **Caring**—Parent(s) tell the child it is important to help other people.
27. **Equality and social justice**—Parent(s) tell the child it is important to speak up for equal rights for all people.
28. **Integrity**—Parent(s) tell the child it is important to stand up for one's beliefs.
29. **Honesty**—Parent(s) tell the child it is important to tell the truth.
30. **Responsibility**—Parent(s) tell the child it is important to accept personal responsibility for behavior.
31. **Healthy Lifestyle**—Parent(s) tell the child it is important to have good health habits and an understanding of healthy sexuality.

Social Competencies
32. **Planning and decision making**—Child thinks about decisions and is usually happy with results of her or his decisions.
33. **Interpersonal Competence**—Child cares about and is affected by other people's feelings, enjoys making friends, and, when frustrated or angry, tries to calm her- or himself.
34. **Cultural Competence**—Child knows and is comfortable with people of different racial, ethnic, and cultural backgrounds and with her or his own cultural identity.
35. **Resistance skills**—Child can stay away from people who are likely to get her or him in trouble and is able to say no to doing wrong or dangerous things.
36. **Peaceful conflict resolution**—Child seeks to resolve conflict nonviolently.

Positive Identity
37. **Personal power**—Child feels he or she has some influence over things that happen in her or his life.
38. **Self-esteem**—Child likes and is proud to be the person that he or she is.
39. **Sense of purpose**—Child sometimes thinks about what life means and whether there is a purpose for her or his life.
40. **Positive view of personal future**—Child is optimistic about her or his personal future.

References

"Anyone Can Mix It Up!" (2008). *Teaching Tolerance*, Fall.

Bloom, Benjamin S. (ed.) (1956). *Taxonomy of Educational Objectives, the Classification of Educational Goals—Handbook I: Cognitive Domain*. New York: McKay.

Chopra, Deepak (1994). *The Seven Spiritual Laws of Success*. San Rafael, California: Amber-Allyn.

Curwin, Richard, and Allen Mendler (1999). *Discipline with Dignity*. Alexandria, Virginia: Association for Supervision and Curriculum Development.

Glasser, William (1984). *Control Theory: A New Explanation of How We Control Our Lives*. New York: Harper and Row.

Glasser, William (1999). *The Quality School: Managing Students without Coercion*. New York: Harper Perennial.

Kohn, Alfie (1995). "Punished by Rewards? A Conversation with Alfie Kohn." *Educational Leadership*, September.

Kohn, Alfie (1999). *Punished by Rewards: The Trouble with Gold Stars, Incentive Plans, A's, Praise, and Other Bribes*. Boston: Houghton Mifflin.

McCarthy, Bernice (2000). *About Learning* (2nd ed.). Wauconda, Illinois: About Learning, Inc.

Nelsen, Jane (1987). *Positive Discipline: A Warm, Practical, Step-by-Step Sourcebook for Parents and Teachers*. New York: Ballantine Books.

Nelsen, Jane, Lynn Lott, and H. Stephen Glenn (1993). *Positive Discipline in the Classroom: How to Effectively Use Class Meetings and Other Positive Discipline Strategies*. Roseville, California: Prima Publishing.

Paley, Vivian Gussin (1992). *You Can't Say You Can't Play*. Cambridge, Massachusetts: Harvard University Press.

Simmons, Rachel (2002). *Odd Girl Out: The Hidden Culture of Aggression in Girls*. New York: Harcourt Books.

Starkman, Neal, Peter C. Scales, and Clay Roberts (2006). *Great Places to Learn* (2nd ed.). Minneapolis, Minnesota: Search Institute Press.

"Teacher Attrition: A Costly Loss to the Nation and to the States" (2005). Alliance for Excellent Education. *Issue Brief*, August.

About the Author

Elizabeth Manvell is a lifelong educator with a master's degree in education and a Certificate of Advanced Study in school and district administration from the State University of New York at Cortland. After a long career in teaching, as an elementary principal and in regional staff development, she most recently served as a college instructor and supervisor for student teachers. Liz now spends her time thinking, researching, and writing about education. She continues to be inspired by the unique role teachers play in the lives of children and families, and by what compassion and tenacity can accomplish on their behalf. Liz has two grown children and enjoys life in Southern California with her husband, Arthur, and their dog and two cats. She is currently working on a history book for students based on original letters from a Civil War soldier and her quest to piece together his life and find his descendants.